Praise for
High Performance Families

Our family has worked with Joanne for several years. She talked with everyone in the family, explored "issues" we didn't know we had, and helped us find solutions we never could have thought of on our own. We're deeply grateful for her insights and her help.

Her new book, High Performance Families, *is not just theory and psychologist-babble. Instead, Joanne shares real stories from real families and shows specific steps they have taken to increase and safeguard their wealth as well as their happiness.*

> – BILL BONNER, Founder and Chairman, Agora Inc.

You hold in your hand a remarkable book. I consider it the families "owner's-manual" that all of us should have been given at birth. Dr. Stern has taken complex relationship matters, removed all the jargon and psycho-babble that drives me crazy, and created a user-friendly guide to fixing broken families or fine-tuning more functional ones with steps that can be implemented immediately.

> – G. JOSEPH MCLINEY, President, McLiney and Company

most definitely do not consider myself the "touchy-feely" type. And many of you who are considering reading this book may not be either. But facts are hard things to ignore. The truth is the overwhelming majority of family wealth is lost due to "soft" issues in our family relationships, not bad investments or poor estate planning.

With clear and engaging writing, High Performance Families *will help you and your family overcome the problems that threaten your family's collective well-being today and its multigenerational legacy for the future. Read it, absorb it, and put its recommendations into action. I think you will be very glad you did.*

> – Kenneth P. Metcalfe, President, The Kenrich Group, LLC

High Performance Families *speaks to the challenges and opportunities that face every family with wealth or a family business, and it does so in a positive and productive way. With short chapters, each beginning with an engaging real-life story and ending with a series of practical suggestions, this book should serve as an invaluable resource for many families and family offices.*

– Dr. Keith Whitaker, President, Wise Counsel Research

Joanne Stern's book is a real gem. It is filled with practical advice for families of wealth, made accessible through countless stories and real-life anecdotes. She clearly has tremendous experience as a psychologist, consultant, parent, and spouse, and she draws on all of that for the benefit of her readers. High Performance Families *tackles difficult issues such as trust between family members, addictions, parent-child struggles, and communication between life partners. These are the very issues that make or break what happens to us in life. I can easily recommend Dr. Stern's book for its wisdom and its heart.*

– James Grubman PhD, Owner,
FamilyWealth Consulting; author of *Strangers in Paradise.
How Families Adapt to Wealth Across Generations*

High Performance Families

PRESERVING WEALTH AND HAPPINESS
FOR GENERATIONS

JOANNE STERN, PhD

CONTENTS

FOREWORD

I n a field that is overwhelmingly qualitative in its measures, we are fortunate to have a handful of definitively quantitative measures at our disposal. Foremost among those is the 2003 book *Preparing Heirs* (Robert D. Reed, San Francisco, California), by Roy Williams and Vic Preisser.

Based on interviews with 3,250 families who had transitioned their wealth, the authors inferred that 70 percent of family succession plans fail, typically due to a breakdown of communication and trust. I'm convinced the problem is even more acute.

After nearly 100 years of combined practice, my father and I put the number at 85 percent, and we take it a step beyond breakdowns of communication and trust. In our estimation, it is the inability to establish a legacy of good joint decision making that most seriously endangers a successful transition of family wealth from one generation to the next.

In the book you are about to read, Joanne Stern offers valuable insight into how families can form the basis for good joint decision making. Through poignant real-life stories, she teaches you how to build excellent communication skills, establish deep trust – founded in consistent, reciprocal responsible behavior – among family members, and prepare rising-generation family members to be great stewards and inheritors, all of which can help your family govern itself well.

High Performance Families is a seriously learned discussion, grounded in Joanne's years of experience as a psychotherapist counseling families, as well as her years as a member of a wealthy family system. All of that has prepared her well for the important task of giving your family a fair chance to be in the 15 percent of families who successfully transition their wealth rather than the 85 percent who fail.

One of her many key observations is that families are composed of four qualitative capitals (human, intellectual, social, and spiritual) and one quantitative capital (financial). She will help you appreciate that a family's success lies in growing the first four capitals – supported by the dynamic preservation of the fifth capital. By growing all five capitals, families can develop a culture that enables them to sustain themselves for multiple generations and thereby meet my definition of a great family.

Great families are those who are capable of adapting to the many threats they will face on their journey. Families who plant trees for younger-generation members to shelter under, the planters knowing they will never see the tree mature. Families who share meaningful stories of their origin to explain whence their defining virtues arise. Families whose elders act as wisdom keepers. Families who focus on the simple task of making more good decisions than bad ones to assure a long future. Families whose culture infuses their structures so they support rather than inhibit flourishing. Families who can repeat the joy of enhancement generation after generation as all family members' individual boats rise together.

We and each of our families are indebted to Joanne for sharing her life and its experience toward helping our families flourish. Thank you, Joanne.

James (Jay) E. Hughes Jr.
Aspen, Colorado, May 2015

INTRODUCTION

As a psychotherapist for many years, I worked with individuals, couples and families in Aspen, Colorado, helping clients mend relationship problems and deal with a wide variety of life transitions, struggles, and tragedies. When I went back to school to earn a PhD in human and organizational systems, I also began to work with businesses at home and abroad, helping them to better understand and strengthen relationships between their people. But no matter how small or how large the corporations I worked with, I came to realize that none were as intricate, as entangled, or as challenging as the family system.

Indeed, families are the most complex organizations in the world.

Why? Because siblings and parents are tied together in layers of strong emotional memories and experiences that don't unravel easily. Because the differences in children appear while they are still young and developing their individual personalities. Because siblings compare themselves to one another. Family members vie for the attention and approval that will make them feel their own worth.

As families grow and expand, priorities change, loyalties shift, and values get tested to the max. Families have to learn to be flexible to incorporate new members and let go after death or divorce. People within a family have a wide range of passions and ambitions that, at times, clash with one another. Family structures are complicated, and siblings can feel threatened and treated unfairly. Family relationships can get fragmented and fraught with conflict. Expectations can be high and disappointments huge – and often unavoidable. Yet, families are sealed with a deep and unique bond.

Healing and strengthening those bonds create enormous benefits for every member of the family. That's why several years ago I began working with entire family systems. I realized how needy and helpless families can be, not having the skills to work through even the most common problems. I began traveling all over the world to help multigenerational families – matriarchs and patriarchs, adult children and their spouses, and even grandchildren – learn ways to repair and stabilize their families.

Over the twenty five years of my career, I have seen how dramatically wealth compounds the complications within families as both parents and children try to manage the intricate interplay between money and work, family and business, values and purpose. Relationships become easily strained because family members don't have the skills to discuss and work through jealousies, sibling rivalries, disagreements, and conflicts. Deeply embedded issues of family dynamics leak out as siblings secretly question if they can match up to their successful parents or achieve as much as their brothers and sisters. Do their parents believe in them? Will they have a chance to hold a position in the family business? Will they be treated fairly or will another sibling take advantage of them? Will they be able to make it in the world without the financial support of parents?

Because parents are uncomfortable talking about their lives or their wealth, they don't share easily with family members. A shroud of secrecy envelops the family and a culture of no information develops. The close connections that siblings had as children loosen. Suspicions and doubts creep in because family members no longer communicate openly. Distrust is only a step behind.

As the problems grow bigger, families collapse, leaving unhappy and broken relationships behind. It's only a matter of time after the relationships are broken that the wealth disappears. That's right. First the relationships, then the money.

Every family I've worked with wants to preserve their wealth.

They have hired platoons of people to manage their financial and legal matters. They want to make sure they've covered every potential danger of loss and found the best ways to protect, grow, and transfer their money. If only these families put the same amount of time, effort, and determination into their family members, they would reap the benefits that money cannot buy – joy and fulfillment. And they would preserve not only their wealth but also their happiness for many generations to come.

The fact is that 70 percent of families (and 90 percent of family businesses) lose their wealth within three generations, as the proverb "shirtsleeves to shirtsleeves in three generations" describes. It is also a fact that no amount of legal counsel, estate planning, or expert wealth management will make your family more likely to be in the 30 percent who preserve their wealth and happiness across generations.

The basic problem is that families lose their wealth because families fall apart.

So what do the 30 percent do that make them successful? They focus on their families. They invest time and resources into people and relationships. They do the hard work necessary to learn about their family dynamics, understand their family problems, and face them head on. They do what it takes to keep their families together. It's not easy to do, but they commit anyway because the alternative is the loss of unity. And loss of wealth follows close behind.

I call these families **High Performance Families**.

High performance families are proactive instead of reactive. They understand that the "shirtsleeves to shirtsleeves" phenomenon does not stem from poor financial planning or bad legal advice. They know they can hire people to invest and manage their money, then sit back and enjoy the fruits of their decisions. But they also realize they have to be intimately involved with their investment in their family.

High performance families notice potential problems – small issues that still hover on the horizon – and they address them before they mushroom into bigger problems. They pay attention to the individuals in their family and take great care in learning about each one in order to give them the attention, encouragement, and support they need to find their way along their life's journey.

They face problems head on. They take the business of building strong, positive relationships seriously. And they engage a professional to help them craft mission statements, family constitutions, and family councils, the structures that will carry their family values and their family members into the future. These high performance families leave behind a legacy of which they can be proud.

High performance families are successful because they are happy, and they actively strive to be that way.

I wrote this book in order to help your family become a high performance family and find the secret to success. If you are willing to do the work, your family will become prosperous long into the future. The secret is simple: Make your family your top priority. The results will be well worth your time and effort.

I have had the privilege of helping many families become high performance families. I bring with me my training and experience in psychology, organization development, family systems theory, group dynamics, and theology to help families. It is an honor to walk into a family's most intimate, private struggles and help them learn the tools and build the roads to get through them. I've helped families address the tough issues of addiction, divorce, and grief and loss from deaths. I've overseen resolutions for sibling rivalries, serious conflicts, poor communication skills, and distrust among siblings and between generations.

I've worked with families to learn how to impart healthy money values and build a positive family culture that will benefit both current and future generations. I've taught skills in maintaining healthy relationships with adult children, dealing with spouses that enter the family system, and bringing younger generations into the family business. I've worked with kids who have grown up in the shadow of their successful parents to help them overcome their issues. Together we've developed the policies and the structures that will sustain the family over generations.

These families are committed to building and maintaining strong family relationships. They are committed despite what can seem at first like insurmountable challenges. They soon come to learn that, although their family struggles may be serious, they are not uncommon, and there are solutions to their problems.

A friend told me recently that he was shocked to hear that wealthy families have problems. He thought that money solved everything. I've heard this opinion over and over. Many people look with envy or even disdain at affluent families. What could they possibly be struggling with?

In reality, all families have problems. It comes with the territory. But affluent families face unique challenges that are often overlooked and misunderstood. In our culture of materialism there is a strong message that money brings happiness. So wealthy families often believe they have no right to be depressed or troubled. Society dismisses their complaints and even scorns them for thinking they could have anything to be unhappy about.

Yet, members of affluent families experience feelings of isolation. Their need for privacy cuts them off from family and friends. In an environment of high productivity, they have little leisure time and no time to relax and release stress. Because they lead busy lives that are filled with obligations, they have less time for socializing and developing personal relationships. Wealth creators may have less time to spend with children and begin to feel inadequate at home. In a highly competitive and visible world, the pressure to attain status can feel intense. Self-doubt, insecurity, and fear of failure creep in. Both parents and children suffer under the strain.

Families of wealth are challenged with these unique problems. But they are tied together in ways that families without wealth are not.

If you were from a family with no significant amount of money, you could just turn your back and walk away from a sibling you didn't like. You could simply decline the invitation to the family Thanksgiving dinner. But when there are family trusts, family philanthropic ventures, a family business – and family decisions to be made about any of those structures – you have to show up. And you bring to the table with you the old hurts from when you were young, all your suspicions and mistrust, your childhood experiences and memories. This is where it can explode as the tangle of deeply rooted emotions comes pouring out, alienating others in the family.

Kids who grow up in affluent families face their own set of problems as they struggle to feel worthy in the presence of high-achieving parents. They often feel alone, neglected, and empty as busy parents fulfill their business and social obligations. The pressure to achieve and excel – sometimes in areas for which they have little interest or passion – crashes down upon them, leaving them in search of meaning and purpose in their lives.

The wake-up call for parents is the astounding and frightening research that shows affluent kids as the new "at risk" kids. They suffer from significantly higher levels of addiction to drugs and alcohol, more symptoms of severe anxiety and deeper depression that can lead to suicide than kids who grow up in poverty in inner-city ghettos!

What seems like paradise on the outside can be painful and threatening on the inside.

These are the circumstances I often walk into when I begin to work with a family. The problems are significant. But with hard work and courage, they can be overcome. It's not the size of the problem but the determination to resolve it that defines a high performance family.

Most parents have good intentions. They want the best for their kids and their entire families. They want family happiness and harmony. They want to leave behind a legacy they can be proud of and that will leave their grandchildren in a position to flourish. They just don't know how to get there. They need professional help to achieve those goals. That's why they come to someone like me.

In my consulting and workshops I get many questions from families about the issues they face. I began writing a series of articles in order to help families better understand themselves, their problems and how to face them. That is the first step toward becoming a high performance family.

This book is a collection of those articles. I have divided them into five sections – relationships, family values, trust and communication, parenting, and family governance. These are the five building blocks of success for high performance families. The articles demonstrate many of the common problems families struggle with in day-to-day life. I examine each problem through real-life stories of clients (with names and circumstances disguised) as well as stories of my own family.

I have found that most families have much in common, regardless of our individual circumstances or economic situations. Deep down inside we're all pretty much the same. Because most families face similar situations and problems, I hope that many of the stories will resonate with you and give you helpful insights into your own family. I hope they will instill in you the courage to take the necessary steps that will develop healthier connections among your family members. I hope this book will lead you into action to improve the trust, communication, and respect among your family members. I hope you will commit to focusing on your family as devotedly as you have on your finances, because it is the best way to secure both your wealth and your personal happiness.

I'm deeply grateful to my clients and to my family members for the opportunities they have given me to grow both personally and professionally. I hope the articles in this book will help you to grow as well.

But learning, change, and growth require action. No amount of talking or understanding will get you to your goals. You may have the best intentions in the world, but until you take action, you can achieve very little. That's why each article includes a step-by-step process for making progress in any area of family life that can improve your family relationships.

May you discover new pathways for creating and maintaining health and prosperity within your family so that you and those you love most will experience greater well-being and happiness. May you find the road toward becoming a high performance family.

Joanne Stern, PhD

Relationships:
The First Building Block of High Performance Families

A good relationship is something to be prized. It's based in mutual respect and trust that is the product of ongoing attention and maintenance. The result is immense pleasure. A good relationship is really a friendship. Not a temporary or volatile friendship, or one in which competition, jealousy, or abandonment seeps in. It's a friendship defined by commitment. Friends don't betray each other, scorn each other, or give bad advice. They stand strong through thick and thin and never give up on the other person. They're there for the long haul and develop a lifelong bond of love and loyalty.

In contrast, weak or broken relationships affect everyone in your family, covering them with a heavy blanket of stress, hurt, and negativity. Everyone suffers when family members don't get along. The bad feelings spill into family get-togethers and activities and prevent the bonding that is essential for long-term family success.

To develop strong positive relationships with your family members, you have to get involved in their lives on a regular basis. You can't just drop in from time to time. They have to know you're there for them – to cheer and to cry, to support and to encourage. You have to let them know you care. You have to share with them as well as listen to them because that's how they know they're important to you. Building relationships means learning to accept and enjoy differences without seeing those differences as a threat. And participating in activities they're interested in even though you are not. You have to let them know how valuable they are.

Relationships can be fragile. When they're strained or broken, you walk on eggshells. Anything you say or do might cause an explosion. But when your connections are strong, you can confront and say the difficult things. You can even practice tough love – as long as you do it sensitively and respectfully.

So, remember the most basic concept of relationship building. It's a simple concept. When a problem or a crisis arises, don't react. Don't panic. First and foremost secure and protect your relationship. Make sure you don't say or do anything that will damage your connection to your family members. Don't walk away. Maintain and even increase your contact. There's plenty of time to solve the problem once your family knows you understand and you're on their side.

Good relationships are the bedrock of your family. They're worth fighting for. But broken ones leave your family without a solid foundation upon which to build. High performance families work hard to maintain close connections because they know their long-term success hinges on the unity and harmony that comes from strong relationships.

CHAPTER 1

Repair Broken Relationships:
Set Your Family on the Track for Success

'd like to tell you about Joe, an entrepreneur whose family I have consulted with.

Joe had created a successful business, built a financial empire, and become recognized as top-notch in his field. He sat on several boards, contributed to worthy causes, and was sought after as a trusted adviser.

His life was full of accomplishments. And I respected him a great deal for what he had been able to achieve.

The only problem was that Joe's marriage was shaky and his kids didn't like him very much at all. Although Joe was Neiman Marcus in his professional life, he was Sears' bargain basement in his personal life.

I reminded Joe that if something didn't shift, there was a good chance he would lose his marriage – which would have devastated him. Furthermore, he didn't have good relationships with his kids. He wasn't close to his grandkids, either. And he'd told me how sad that was for him.

He was about to lose everything that mattered most to him because he had poor relationships with his family.

But there was good news for Joe, as there is for anyone else who finds himself in a similar boat. If you put the same passion, focus, and commitment into your family relationships as you did into your business, you'll be able to create a happy and fulfilling family life. You'll be Neiman Marcus all around.

You probably already have everything it takes. It requires nothing more than simple adjustments to your attitude and your priorities.

And you're in charge of both...

The Pressures of a Busy Life

The family wealth creator often stays late at the office, works weekends, travels for business... and is preoccupied when he's at home.

And when his wife complains that he's never there for her... that he doesn't take time to share feelings... and that she feels like she's way down on his priority list, he tells her she is ungrateful – or at least that she doesn't understand.

After all, he's doing all of this for *her* – to provide for her and their kids the lifestyle they have come to expect.

The kids don't really know their dad because he never took the time to get to know them. He neglected to talk with them when they were growing up. He didn't plan his schedule to include their school activities and sports events.

Whenever they *did* ask him something, he was too busy to put down what he was doing and look at them. They never knew if he was really listening or if he even cared. So now that they're adults, they've gone their own ways, because there was no real draw from home to keep them pulled together or close-knit as a family.

If you don't have close relationships within your family, you won't become a high performance family. You're at much greater risk of losing your wealth because family members won't be able to come together to make good decisions. Family happiness will become a distant memory because tension, distrust, and conflict will replace the harmony you yearn for.

A Family Breaks Apart

Not long ago, Carlos told me his family story. Carlos was one of three sons whose father had built a very successful manufacturing company in Argentina. Carlos had a degree in engineering and worked in the family business. His two brothers didn't work but played polo instead. At the end of the year, all three sons received the same distribution.

After a couple of years Carlos became irritated that he worked every day and got the same compensation as his two brothers who played every day. So he went to his father and asked for a salary. His father said, "Ridiculous! Of course, you're getting paid. Everyone in the family is getting paid."

So Carlos continued to talk with his father and his family about his complaint, to no avail. The relationships in the family weren't strong enough to support this kind of difficult conversation. Instead of solving the problem, family members became tense, irritated, and obstinate. Relationships became strained, and arguments broke out.

Carlos decided to leave the family business and work for another company where he would get paid for his expertise. After one year, Carlos received the same distribution from his family – and he also received a handsome salary from the company he was working for. But his family had seen a decline, because Carlos had been one of the principal contributors to the success of their business.

His father asked him to come back. Again, Carlos asked to be paid for his work, but he got the same answer. He went back to work, but during that year he identified four people to whom he could sell his shares of stock. By the end of the year Carlos had divested himself of all of his family stock, and four outsiders now owned one fourth of the family business.

Carlos left the family company and bid goodbye to his family.

The Road to Success

Carlos' family is now at great risk of demonstrating the "shirt-sleeves to shirtsleeves in three generations" proverb. Once relationships are broken and family has fallen apart, the money is very likely to dissipate.

Studies show that 70 percent of families lose their ability to transfer their wealth beyond three generations, not because of poor legal or financial advice but because of poor family relationships.

Every family has to be able to talk through the difficult issues that come up. You have to have strong enough and positive enough relationships within the family to be able to dig in and work through the tough stuff. Otherwise, family members leave, sabotage the family business, disrupt family meetings, rebel against family decisions, become indifferent, make poor decisions, and a host of other negative actions that undermine the success of your family.

Good relationships put you on the road to success. The 30 percent of families who succeed in being able to transfer wealth for many generations have made positive relationships a top priority. Members of these families learn to communicate effectively with one another, build trust, and confront uncomfortable subjects. They have relationships that are grounded in respect, understanding, and genuine caring for one another.

What to Do Next...

Building a strong family system that is poised for high performance constitutes a series of action steps. The first step is to ensure that your own relationships with family members are solid. Only then can you begin to address the relationships of the others in your family.

These are some of the things you can do to repair and renew your family relationships:

1. **Have the courage to address issues honestly.** Don't live in denial, thinking that problems will go away on their own. If you talk with each family member individually and explain that you want to grow a new family culture that values harmony and close family ties, they're likely to come on board. After all, they want family happiness too.

2. **Learn to listen.** Even small children like to be heard. It shows respect for your family members, regardless of their ages and levels of life experience. Sometimes it's hard to listen because you may think the other person isn't telling the facts accurately or remembering the incidents correctly. Maybe you think they're distorting reality. But you don't have to agree. You just have to listen and accept the perspectives and feelings of the other person.

3. **Be willing to apologize.** You're not always right, and your family members know it. If you've been negligent about spending time with them or if you've behaved in a way you're not proud of, tell them. Accept responsibility for your part of the broken relationship and develop a willingness to change your behavior and your priorities.

4. **Make a commitment to instigate more open communication within the family and to practice more mutual sharing.** This means a give-and-take of information, feelings, and opinions. Don't just impose your beliefs on everyone else in your family. Let them know you value what they have to say. Be open to hearing what they think and eager to discuss their ideas.

5. **Back off on criticism and judgment.** Nothing shuts down a relationship more quickly. No one likes to be criticized, demeaned, or belittled – not at any age. Even years later you may not remember what was said, but you will remember how you

felt when someone made you feel wrong, bad, or inadequate. It's a relationship killer.

6. **Spend more time with your family** – one on one and as a group – and develop positive, meaningful relationships with each member, your kids as well as your spouse. You don't build relationships from a distance. It takes time and face-to-face interaction. Take interest in their passions, become involved in their lives, and participate in their activities. Relationships are a contact sport!

7. **Accept that it might take time.** Be patient. If your relationships are weak or broken, you can't rebuild them overnight. It's well worth getting professional help. No amount of money can overcome the deficit of bad relationships. And nothing is more valuable than getting your family on track with healthy relationships.

At first, all of this might seem too difficult – too time-consuming, and too uncomfortable. But with determination you will gradually begin to experience the rewards of your efforts.

As you make progress, you will come to believe, as other successful families have, that the value of family bonding, mutual support, and caring is greater than the value of your portfolio.

Remember, it's never too late to rebuild, renew, or refresh relationships in your family. They greatly increase your chances of maintaining and growing your family wealth and providing the harmony, unity, and goodwill that brings fulfillment and happiness for a lifetime.

Good family relationships may be the best legacy you could ever leave behind.

CHAPTER 2

Build Stronger Connections:
Don't Get Hijacked by Assumptions

The Billings family was at a crossroads.

The matriarch and patriarch had recently died. The family's oldest son, Dan, had taken over as CEO of the family business when he made an important decision...

The Billings were a secretive clan. They didn't communicate well. And Dan wanted to change that.

So he invited his family members to learn more about the family enterprises and their trusts. To start, Dan asked his nieces and nephews to compile a list of questions for him to address at the next family meeting.

Dan's family members welcomed his move. They were proud of their family business. They were excited to learn more about it and have input on its future. They were eager to understand the structure of the family trusts. They wanted to become respected and responsible stewards of their family's wealth...

So they put together a list of questions and gave it to Dan a month before the meeting to give him time to prepare.

But when the list landed on Dan's desk, he panicked.

That's because, eight years earlier, Dan's brother had given him a list of questions on similar topics that had caused havoc in the family business...

A Critical Misjudgment

Dan's brother had sent him a list of questions about loopholes in the trusts and the valuation of the family business. He had threatened lawsuits, accused trustees and family attorneys of misdeeds, and created turmoil in the business for more than a year. And although he dropped his threats after his concerns were addressed, he walked away from the family. He hasn't connected with anyone in the family since.

When Dan received the questions from his nieces and nephews, he made a big mistake. He assumed that his brother had come out of hiding and was colluding with them to bring instability to the family business.

When his nieces and nephews arrived at the family meeting, Dan came across as distant and secretive. They couldn't understand what had caused such a drastic change in him. He had gone from inclusive to off-putting.

Dan responded in businesslike fashion to their list of questions. But his entire demeanor had changed...

What happened to the guy who had wanted to bring transparency to his family?

Dan held tightly to his assumption that his brother was colluding with his nieces and nephews. His actions told them he didn't trust them. And now they didn't trust him either. They felt disrespected and suspicious. They weren't sure how they wanted to proceed with him and the business.

Over time, his nieces and nephews began to learn of the history between Dan and his brother. They explained to him that their questions were unrelated to his brother's. But Dan couldn't hear them. His ability to listen was blocked by his assumptions. He decided to jump to a conclusion and stick with what he already believed.

Dan's is a cautionary tale about the consequences of jumping to conclusions without verifying the truth of your assumptions. When you assign bad motives to the actions of others based on assumptions, you create distrust. And once trust leaves a family, it is extremely hard to recover. Family connections get severed – sometimes irreparably.

Breach of Faith

One afternoon, fifteen-year-old Katrina asked her mom to drive her to town to hang out with friends. When her mom said she was too busy, Katrina got angry and bolted out of the house. She was gone in a flash.

Katrina's mom and dad were worried that she was hitchhiking to town – something that they forbade. It was too far to walk. And her dad's cellphone was missing. They thought she had taken it to contact her friends on the way. So the parents jumped in the car to find her – but couldn't.

Katrina's parents returned home to get ready for a dinner out with friends. When they left, they locked Katrina out of the house as punishment. What they didn't know was that Katrina was merely walking in the woods behind their home to release some of her anger. She had not taken her dad's cellphone. (He later found it in his jacket pocket.) She had not hitchhiked to town.

Katrina returned home just before dark to a locked house. She found an open window and climbed inside. Her parents returned a couple of hours later. Katrina was watching TV in the living room feeling furious, unjustly treated and betrayed.

But even when Katrina explained where she had been, her parents didn't apologize. They felt justified in their actions because she had done irrational things in the past.

Now Katrina believed her parents didn't trust her at all. She was angry and felt betrayed. She couldn't believe they had jumped to conclusions before finding out the truth from her. This caused a serious breach of faith that damaged their relationship.

Stuck in Reverse

When Ed and Amy came to see me, they were on the brink of divorce. They had developed some bad relationship habits. Each judged the other on past behaviors. And no matter what progress each had made in changing bad behaviors, they continued to see each other through the prism of the past.

When Ed called Amy to tell her he would be home from the office in an hour, she ragged on him for being a half-hour late. She greeted him at the door with a sarcastic remark about how he must have stayed at the office to have a drink with his buddy – like he used to do. In truth, Ed had received an important business call just as he was walking out the door.

But Ed wasn't an innocent party. When Amy walked in the house with a shopping bag, he accused her of spending money though they had agreed to be thrifty. Ed assumed she was ignoring their agreement. But Amy's bag was just filled with clothes she was bringing back from the tailor.

The old memories that Amy and Ed had stored away tainted the way they saw the present. They were quick to act on assumptions based on past behavior. And they regularly criticized each other without checking whether their assumptions were true. These actions nearly destroyed their marriage.

Leave the Past Behind

We all make assumptions in life. If my husband remembered my birthday last year, I assume he will remember it again this year. If he forgot it last year, I'll be concerned that he'll forget it again this year. That's just human nature.

It's hard to let go of an assumption. But when you expect current behavior to duplicate past behavior, you can make inaccurate judgments. And assumptions put people in a box and don't give them the benefit of the doubt to do things differently.

But making assumptions is one thing. The real damage is done when you act on those assumptions and treat people as if they will automatically behave as they did in the past. When you jump to a conclusion without verifying the truth of your assumption, you create distrust and ill will.

In relationships, it's important to clear your mind of preconceived notions and give others a chance to be different. When you expect the same old thing over and over, you usually get exactly that. But when you expect something different – something better – you often get that instead.

Whenever you find yourself jumping to conclusions, remember these three tips:

1. **Find out the truth before you say or do anything that could create distrust or damage a relationship.** You are not prepared to reach a conclusion or make a judgment until you know the facts.

2. **Don't allow your memories from the past to taint what can happen in the future.** People *do* change their attitudes and their behaviors, and they want to be given a chance to act differently.

3. **Celebrate new behaviors as though you expected them.** Your acceptance helps generate the impetus for those behaviors to become the new norm.

Tension, conflict, and distrust fester in families when inaccurate assumptions hijack relationships. Healthy families allow goodwill and harmony to grow by giving family members the benefit of the doubt.

If you let go of old assumptions and give your family members the chance to grow, you'll be amazed at what you discover. The connections will grow stronger and family members will become closer. This doesn't mean you won't be disappointed by the repeated behavior of loved ones from time to time. You will. But you'll be building far more positive relationships when your family members realize you always approach them with an open mind and you aren't holding past behaviors against them.

CHAPTER 3

Learn to Fight Fair:
Practicing the Skills of a Pro

Anybody can lose their cool, blow up, and yell…

But it takes skill to have a productive fight and come out with a positive result on the other end. You need tools to argue so that you don't damage your relationship in the middle of a quarrel.

Marilyn and Robert started to argue while discussing a marital problem in my office. Marilyn began by stating that Robert didn't accept his share of the responsibility around the home. He didn't help her with household tasks and he didn't help their daughter with her homework. She couldn't even count on him to be home from work in time for dinner.

As she talked, her voice grew louder.

Since Robert was feeling attacked, he began to defend himself heatedly and threw in a few jabs at his wife at the same time.

The argument escalated in a flash. Enraged, Marilyn started shouting as though her decibel level would ensure her winning. She spewed out a litany of other unrelated accusations, even something he had done before their daughter was born. She called her husband a lazy, self-centered bum she never should have married. She even threw in a snide remark about how he could never do things right, even if he tried. Marilyn was already out of control before I could stop her tirade.

Robert slumped down in quiet defeat, but the damage was done.

It would take work to repair the harm Marilyn had caused to their relationship.

An Argument Derailed

Marilyn and Robert's argument is an example in which almost everything went wrong. Within the space of a few sentences, their argument flew off the tracks.

- **The element of attack and defend took over.** Marilyn's attack was degrading to the Robert. Feeling criticized, condemned and verbally assaulted, Robert's natural tendency was to defend himself. In defense mode, you can't hear what your partner is saying because you're busy trying to survive the attack. There's no possibility of resolving an issue with this approach.

- **Marilyn threw in the kitchen sink.** By accusing Robert of unrelated behaviors and bringing up events from the past, she diverted the attention of both of them from the issues she was upset about. In a kitchen sink argument, no one remembers what the original grievance was even about. Without focus on the primary complaint, there is little hope of coming up with ideas to solve anything.

- **Marilyn tried to control Robert with her anger.** Her method was the heavy control of blame, criticism, and put-downs. Like many people, Marilyn thought that control could be effective. By blaming him and making him feel bad about how he had neglected her, she thought he would change and start doing what she wanted him to. There are other forms of heavy control including name-calling, judging, demanding, lying, and ordering. But subtler styles of control, such as denying, nagging, withholding, foot-dragging, and excuses can be just as injurious. And none of them work. No one wants to be controlled, either aggressively or passively. Attempts to control lead to a pulling away from the other person and from the problem. Nothing gets settled when control is at play.

- **Both Robert and Marilyn allowed their emotions to fly out of control.** Anger is an intense feeling and it's okay to express that intensity. But you cannot yell, use bad language, or make disrespectful comments. You cannot hit below the belt, making comments that attack your partner's personality. Dumping your anger on the other person without regard for their feelings is a demonstration of your own immaturity, not an example of your power. Allowing your feelings to come out indiscriminately is the fastest way to turn an argument into a disaster and the best way to ensure that nothing useful will result.

- **Marilyn used sarcasm and cynicism to make her points.** In the process, she assassinated Robert's character. These two tactics, especially when used habitually, are predictors of relationship failure. According to John Gottman, relationship expert and author of *The Seven Principles for Making Marriage Work*, these are forms of contempt. Contempt is poisonous to a relationship because it conveys disgust. In the midst of sarcasm and cynicism, an argument will not have a positive outcome. Even worse, the relationship can become damaged beyond repair.

Protect the Relationship

Fighting is not necessarily an indication of a bad relationship. In fact, it can be an opportunity to resolve conflicts and grow closer. The principles are the same with your children as with your spouse.

A former client recently called and reminded me of conversations we had had several years ago. He'd separated from his wife and was experiencing the wrath of a teenage son who was rude and insolent with him, blaming him for ripping the family apart.

My client had been so upset by his son's angry accusations that he wanted to yell back at him. He was tempted to exert his power as a father by threatening to kick his son out of the house. He wanted to demean his son by telling him he was too immature to understand. And he wanted to demand respectful behavior, or else.

My client reminded me that I had given him some good advice back then.

I had said, no – do not act on your emotions or mimic your son's outbursts or you will surely regret it. Step up to the plate and act like an adult instead of like your child. Both you and your son are going through a tough time. He has a right to his anger. He just needs to learn how to express it appropriately. Responding inappropriately will push him away.

I encouraged him to use the tools of a pro and teach his son what was and was not acceptable behavior. I asked him to listen attentively so that he could understand his son's anger.

I told him to tell his son that if things got too hot he would leave the room and come back when they were both calmer.

Above all, I urged him to protect and nurture the relationship. Even in the middle of a fight your kids will remember how you treated them. They'll discover whether they can trust you to handle their complaints and work toward resolution.

This is your chance to make your relationship closer.

My client reconnected to tell me he was glad he had heeded my advice. He was grateful that he had learned these tips on how to handle a fight with his son instead of being diverted by his own rash emotions. They developed a wonderfully close and caring relationship that carried them though their pain and chaos and is very fulfilling to both of them today.

A Volcano About to Explode

Now, sometimes you may be so hot under the collar that you just have to blow out. You feel like a volcano that's about to explode and you can't control the lava flow.

This isn't a fight, and you shouldn't treat it like one. This is your own emotional overload and you should keep it to yourself. Don't expect or demand a discussion when you're in this mood. It won't go anywhere but sideways. Instead, go for a run, hit a punching bag, rip newspapers, journal – whatever helps get the feelings out in a nondestructive way.

Even if you're angry with your spouse or your child, remember that the anger belongs to you. Don't expect them to accept your eruption of feelings magnanimously. As with most explosions, it's not a pretty sight, and most people prefer to be far away when it happens.

You can ask permission of your spouse to spew. But you cannot explode without permission or it would feel like a lion springing from behind. Taking someone by surprise is not a healthy way to deal with your anger.

Getting rid of your anger in this way requires a ritual with a clear understanding of boundaries and rules. I strongly recommend that you engage a professional to help you determine how best to handle this kind of intense emotional release so as not to damage your relationships.

Fighting Fair

Dirty fighting is not respectful to your partner, and it doesn't create a pathway for positive change. If you have a legitimate complaint and would like to seek a change of behavior in your spouse, child, or colleague, here are six steps that will lead you to your goal:

1. **Ask permission to address your issue.** Choose an appropriate time and place so that each of you can devote your full attention to the problem. You may have to wait an hour, a day, or

longer to find a good time to talk. Even when you're upset, you can't expect the other person to drop what he or she is doing to accommodate you.

2. **State only one complaint and state it specifically.** It's enough to address only one issue at a time. More than that will be confusing and divert both of you from the topic. Additional complaints from the past tend to rile up old emotions that are detrimental to the discussion.

3. **Make sure your complaint has been clearly understood.** Ask your partner to repeat what you have said. If there is any confusion, clear it up before proceeding. Make sure you are both talking about exactly the same issue.

4. **Make a specific request for change in your partner's behavior.** Remember that stating a complaint without making a reasonable request for change is nothing more than a dump of your feelings. Until you ask for something to change, it is unlikely that your partner will do anything differently.

5. **Wait for your partner's response.** He (or she) may need time to think about what he is willing to do. Be patient with the response time. You have been thinking about your complaint but your partner has not. If he is not willing to do exactly what you ask, be ready to negotiate a compromise. Continue the process until a solution is reached.

6. **Thank your partner for listening to your complaint and for making the commitment to change.** By being respectful and appreciative, you build goodwill and strengthen your relationship.

Notice that, in a fair fight, emotions do not overtake the conversation. In a fair fight, issues are presented and discussed rationally. It's okay to have strong feelings about an issue, but you must deal with the intensity of your emotions *before* you come to the table with your partner. Otherwise you'll derail the conversation and damage your relationship.

Winning is not about one-upmanship. An argument is an opportunity to get to a better relationship. It means you have successfully cleared the air because you've dealt honestly with real issues. There is increased understanding between the two of you. If you've followed the rules and taken the precautions, both people generally feel better about themselves – and about each other.

CHAPTER 4

Deal with Addiction:
How to Wake Up from the Nightmare

A ddiction is a disease of loss. Addicts lose health, money, careers, relationships – and even their lives. It's a family disease, so their families lose as well. It's hard to think of an issue more likely to wreck a family fortune.

Having had personal experience of just how damaging it can be to any family, I often talk with people about the disease of addiction.

Almost everyone knows an alcoholic or a drug addict. They want to know what addiction is, why addicts can't stop using and what collateral damage there could be for the families of substance abusers. And what they can do to help.

Maybe you have an addict in your family. If so, then you have experienced the fear, chaos, and damage that the disease drags along with it.

Addiction seeks no particular socioeconomic level. It is as prevalent in families of wealth as it is in poorer families. Perhaps even more so.

Regardless of where you are on the wealth ladder, addiction destroys. It destroys individual lives and entire families. It eventually takes everything away. It adds nothing but pain, financial ruin, emotional distress... even death.

Unaddressed addiction in your family is a major threat not only to your family wealth but also to your family health. Addiction – even if it affects only one family member – can lead your family into a downward spiral from which you may never recover.

Stephen and Tom

Stephen took his first drink when he was eight. He drained the wineglasses left over from his parents' party and got drunk. Even though he was sick, he told me many years later in therapy that he remembered loving the high he felt.

His parents were unaware. They were often busy and out of town, so he was raised by nannies. In order to feel loved and accepted as an adolescent, he found a group of boys who took him in. At first, these kids drank only on weekends. Then they started drinking during the week. They added pot to the mix and soon after, cocaine. Stephen was addicted by the time he graduated from high school.

For some, addiction takes years to develop. In Stephen's case, it took only months.

Tom is an example in which addiction took longer to take its toll. Like most of his friends, he started drinking in high school at weekend parties. He learned how he felt after one drink... and how he felt after three. He learned how he felt if he drank on an empty stomach and how different it was after dinner. He learned that his personality changed after a couple of drinks and that he felt more comfortable in his skin and more confident with girls.

He learned that alcohol was his friend – trustworthy and dependable – because it worked every time.

The First Three Phases of Addiction

Tom was going through Phase One of Addiction: "Learning the Mood Swings."

In college Tom did well. By his senior year he noticed that instead of a couple of beers on Friday nights, he now drank a six-pack. He was also smoking pot on weekends and several times during the week to take the edge off his stress. He didn't worry about it because most of his friends were doing the same thing, or worse.

After college he got a job and met a girl who introduced him to cocaine. He quickly incorporated coke into his routine because he loved the quick high and, after all, his friends were doing it too.

As the next decade rolled by, Tom began to drink at lunch. Before a weekend barbecue he started drinking after breakfast. Sometimes, he took a bottle of booze to bed to sip before he went to sleep. He was also using cocaine more frequently but saw it as recreational use.

Over time, friends noticed Tom was only interested in events where he could drink. He often stopped off at a bar after work, causing him to be late for dinner. The excuses became more common. He had more hangovers, forgot a couple of his son's soccer games, and started arguments with his wife. But Tom was a charming, good-natured guy. And he was always able to patch things up. So he kept drinking and using because the high was worth the occasional painful consequences.

Tom was racing down the spectrum of Phase Two of Addiction: "Seeking the Mood Swing." He was gradually becoming more and more habituated, but he could still control his consumption.

Tom could have quit. But he didn't.

By the time Tom reached his mid-thirties he had crossed the line into Phase Three of Addiction: "Harmful Dependency."

His lifestyle had now changed. He became preoccupied with the use of his chemicals. Tom began to alter his activities. Instead of rising early on Saturdays to play his favorite sports or spend time with his kids, he stayed in bed nursing a hangover.

He got two DUIs and had an accident he swore was not his fault. His boss told him he had to shape up or he would be fired. He shrugged his shoulders and told his wife the boss had it in for him.

He avoided old friends and started hanging out with new ones, people who drank and used drugs as much as he did. Tom's wife found cocaine hidden in his jacket pockets, in dresser drawers, and on shelves in the garage. He denied it was his and blamed her for snooping.

Tom started having affairs. He lied to his wife about where he had been when he came home late. He verbally attacked her every time she raised her concerns. His value system had gone down the drain.

He was crusty and belligerent on the outside, but on the inside he was hurting. Self-hatred mounted as everything in his life began to spiral downward – relationships, money, health, social life, and spirituality.

He convinced himself and others he could quit if he wanted to. But he couldn't. He had lost control.

The Final Phase

Tom remembered the days when using drugs was fun. But now pleasure was only a distant memory. The more he drank, the more guilt, shame, and hopelessness he felt. As many alcoholics say, "I drink because I'm unhappy. I'm unhappy because I drink."

Tom became a victim of his own defense system. He was now lying to himself. That is the core of addiction.

Tom is one of the lucky ones. His wife contacted someone to conduct an intervention and he went to a treatment center. When I worked with Tom he was clean and sober, trying to rebuild his life.

Many people are not so lucky. They progress even further along the spectrum of the disease until they finally reach Phase Four of Addiction: "Chronic Addiction."

All the feelings and symptoms of Phase Three are heightened, including a total sense of worthlessness, depression, and despair. Severe medical problems arise. The death of their values and morals results in behaviors that make them almost unrecognizable to loved ones.

Interestingly, because tolerance decreases in Phase Four, the addict drinks less than he used to. Don't be fooled: In the late stages of alcoholism, it takes less alcohol to get drunk than it did in the earlier, social drinking stage.

In the end, the addict loses everything. Even his life.

It is difficult to understand how someone could continue to use alcohol and drugs even in the face of death. But that is what addicts do.

Why? Because addiction can be thought of as a brain "disease." In addition to having a genetic component, it disrupts the cortex, that part of the brain responsible for making good decisions. It affects the limbic system, the part of the brain involved in storing and recalling memories, feeling emotions, and recognizing a sense of reward. It upsets the ability to handle stress. And it unravels multiple brain functions that are intended to work together.

In the early stages of drinking, alcohol makes most people feel happier and more relaxed. The drink feels like a positive reward. But in the later stages, the brain becomes reprogrammed. Addicts crave a drug that leads to self-destruction.

Because their brains have become altered, you cannot reason with an addict. They will do almost anything to protect their ability to use their substance of choice.

In the 1950s the American Medical Association described addiction as:

1. **A primary disease** – It is not caused by any other illness.

2. **A progressive disease** – As the illness progresses, it demands more consumption to get the same result.

3. **A chronic disease** – You can be in recovery, but you are never recovered.

4. **A fatal disease** – Addicts die of overdoses, medical problems, accidents and through suicide.

The Road to Recovery

Addiction causes a great deal of collateral damage within a family. Even preverbal children can be negatively affected. As addiction progresses, families get sucked into the vortex and experience their own version of physical, mental, social, emotional, and spiritual decline.

Addiction destroys family wealth and, more importantly, family happiness. Relationships with spouses and children get torn to shreds – often too far gone to repair.

Family members are often just as affected and need help stopping enabling behaviors, understanding unhealthy family dynamics, and learning how to heal from their pain.

Recovery begins with an admission of powerlessness. Addicts are powerless over their substances. Likewise, family members are powerless over the addict. It is only when the addict realizes that he cannot control himself that he can begin to get well.

I have personally experienced the devastation of alcoholism and drug addiction. My two daughters and I stumbled through several years of craziness before my ex-husband became clean and sober. There were times when I thought this could not possibly be my life. I prayed I would wake up from the horror of my nightmare.

But it continued until I finally realized I needed help.

With support and help from friends, we got my ex-husband into a hospital... and from there into a treatment center. But he soon went back to using, even more destructively than before. Two years later, we got him into treatment for a second time. This time I went with him.

I knew I needed to learn about this dreadful disease. I wanted to support him, to help my children, and to heal myself. It was one of the most difficult and humbling experiences I have ever had. But I am grateful for what I've learned. My daughters and I are thriving and my ex-husband has thanked me for saving his life.

You can take these steps if you're facing addiction in your family:

1. **Learn about the disease.** Read books and talk with professionals in the field. Go to Al-Anon. Addiction is cunning, baffling, and powerful. You cannot deal with something so complicated without understanding it.

2. **Don't allow denial to overcome your common sense.** It's scary to face the behaviors you see in your loved one and to acknowledge the reality of the moral, physical, social, and spiritual decline. But if you play into the denial that is a common aspect of addiction, it will only get worse.

3. **Identify how you and your family have changed to accommodate the crazy behavior of your loved one.** Your family's health and well-being is as important as that of the addict. Don't ignore signs and symptoms of dysfunction in you and your children as all of you struggle to make sense of your lives in an out-of-control household.

4. **Seek professional help early.** You cannot do this one on your own. First, try to get help for your loved one. But if the addict is unwilling to seek treatment, make sure you get help for the rest of you. Both you and your children need help to recover from this family disease.

5. **Understand that the health and well-being of your family is at stake.** Relationships that can either make or break you family for many generations are being threatened. Take action before it's too late.

Family Values:
The Second Building Block of
High Performance Families

Families often think in terms of the hard structures and the soft structures they put into place to maintain their family and their family wealth. Your family attorneys, accountants, estate planners, investment advisers, and wealth managers handle the hard structures. You can give them your financial data and your desires for growing and preserving wealth, then sit back and wait for them to present the options for you to reach your goals.

Setting up the soft structures is more difficult because no one can do it for you. You can't simply write a check and expect your kids to develop the characteristics you want them to live by. It doesn't work for someone else to craft a mission statement for your family or write a plan for how your family culture should be. Only you can tell the stories and the history of your family that bind you together as a unique group and create the legacy that will be passed down for generations. You're the only one who can sit down with your kids and talk to them about the value of relationships in your life, what fills you with meaning and purpose, and what you believe about money.

Your family values shape your behaviors. They include how you treat one another and how you interact with your community and the world. Your values dictate your family decisions in business as well as in your personal and social lives. The values of your family will direct your children in the friends they hang out with, the careers they pursue and the partners they choose. Your values will spill onto your grandchildren and determine, in part, the people they will become.

You cannot teach values without being intricately involved in the process. Being involved means that you spend time with family members, modeling the lifestyle you believe in. And it means that you talk with your spouse and your children – individually and as a group – sharing visions, hopes, and dreams for your future.

You sit around the dining room table, you go on family outings, you plan family meetings – events that give you opportunities to talk together as a family. And you tell each other what's important to you, what isn't working, and how you want your family to change and improve.

Through these intentional family get-togethers, families identify and establish values. It's during these occasions that family members bond and feel a sense of being part of a team that holds them together even through the tough times. The process is even more important than the product because family members realize that they benefit more from the discussions and the sharing than they do from the decisions they make.

High performance families know that values are the touchstones of their lives and that strong family values are what make them successful. They don't leave it to chance, allowing outside influences to divert the family from its goals. They work with intention to impart the values they believe in and then live in accordance with those values.

CHAPTER 5

Tell Your Story:
The Ingredient That Binds Your Family Together

Many families want to know if there is a critical ingredient that can make their family successful, resilient, and happy. Perhaps a secret sauce that will hold their family together.

That secret sauce may be as simple as telling stories.

This may sound strange. But research shows that families who talk about their past and tell family stories are healthier than those who do not. Storytelling helps create a strong family narrative that binds families together during the tough times and allows them to feel more connected during the good times.

Families who tell stories also handle challenges more effectively and work harder to resolve conflicts. Family members feel a sense of belonging to something bigger and more significant than themselves. They are more likely to feel proud about where they came from. And this makes them want to pass on those feelings to their children.

These are the families who build true legacies... and cease being ordinary families and become multigenerational family systems.

"Dry Ice" Martinis

Last year, I was consulting with a family who wanted help in identifying their family values. Their parents had died. Thus, they were embarking on their family wealth project without their parents' support.

One of them mentioned the annual camping trips they went on when they were kids. The siblings in the room broke into wide grins. I suddenly felt a bit excluded – I was not a part of something that awoke such strong memories in each of them.

One by one, they began to bring me into their loop... explaining the details of these remarkable excursions into the mountains. Their mom began planning and packing two weeks in advance. They brought along several horses with panniers loaded with gear and food. With chuckles, they recalled the shower tent with its special sun-heated water bag... the ice packed in dry ice for their dad's afternoon martinis... and the fuss over the elaborate, gourmet meals.

They told me how many extra people they included on the trips just to help set up camp and break it down. All of this for just two nights on the forest floor. With big smiles on their faces, they assured me I was lucky to have missed these outings. But, clearly, this was a memory that bonded them.

Of course, lots of families reminisce about the fun they had together as a family. In itself it's nothing special. The real value of this story is how the family had *institutionalized* it as part of the family legacy. The grandkids immediately wanted to reinstate the infamous camping trips. And who can blame them? It gave them an insight into their grandparents to whom they no longer had access but whose memories they wanted to carry into the future.

Untied from the Past

That's why one of the first things you must do, as you begin building a stronger family, is to get to know about your family. If you don't know about your family, you can't know why your family matters. And if you don't know why your family matters, you're not going to inspire anyone to help you make it last.

Simple things like learning where your ancestors were born and how they grew up... how your parents met... and where they went to school... help give your kids a sense of their roots. In a world that is spinning faster than anyone can keep up with, it gives kids of all ages a feeling of being grounded and connected.

This is not my opinion. Studies have shown that the more children know about their family's history, the better prepared they are to handle difficulties and bounce back from stumbling blocks. They have higher self-esteem. This supports them in making tough decisions in life and being self-reliant. And they show greater respect for their parents and grandparents because they understand the challenges their ancestors overcame in creating their successes.

I recently talked with a middle-aged man – let's call him Henry – who is helping to care for his aged mother. She has Alzheimer's disease and is no longer able to converse about her life in a meaningful way.

Although Henry was raised with wealth, he realizes he does not know the contributions made by his maternal grandparents. He does not even know their names. (Because there was tension between his mother and her parents, she never wanted to talk about them.)

Now, that information is lost. And Henry feels he is floating in the unknown. Untied from his past, he feels insecure about his future.

Don't Be Afraid of Failure

There's another big benefit of telling family stories: Knowing where you came from helps to develop appreciation for what you have.

When we were young, my dad used to tell us stories about his childhood. He was raised on a farm in the Midwest in a family that worked hard to provide for him and his ten brothers and sisters.

Every morning he woke up at 6 a.m. to milk cows before going to school. He told us that, one Christmas, he got only a small toy horn and an orange in his Christmas stocking because that was all his parents could afford. When he decided to further his education, his father made fun of him by calling him a "college dude."

My dad told me that he decided two things: He would provide for his children better than his father had provided for him. And he would treat his children more lovingly than he had been treated.

I used to sit in awe as my parents told me about their picnics when they were first married, where they would count the pennies they had saved that week. *I realized it was determination and hard work that created my dad's success.*

Although I often feel sad about my dad's early years, it is important for me to know about them. I am even more grateful for how I grew up. My children listen wide-eyed to the stories of their grandpa and respect and honor him for what he became on his own. They feel proud of him and proud to be a part of our larger family.

Where Families Go Wrong

This is where some families go wrong. They only tell the stories of family successes. But the healthiest family narratives include ups and downs... successes and failures.

This makes sense. Younger generations need to learn that their ancestors experienced setbacks as well as victories. Maybe there was humiliation, emotional trauma, or defeat.

Perhaps someone in the family was exposed negatively in the newspaper in a way that hurt his reputation or that of the family business. Occasional crises and disasters may be a part of the story that eventually led to achievement. This is important information for descendants to know as they struggle through the mazes of their own lives.

Younger generations also need to be aware of the personalities of their grandparents. In one family I've worked with, everyone knew the story of the business their grandfather had founded. That is where their money comes from today. But they knew nothing about the story of the man behind the business. When they learned about his humanitarian contributions and the reputation he had earned in his personal life, they were much more impressed. These stories brought the family together emotionally and created a new commitment to carry on the personal legacy of their grandfather.

Tell Your Stories

Elders, those in the oldest generation, provide an essential role in storytelling. They know the family history better than anyone else. They are able to keep the old stories vibrant for posterity and perpetuate activities for creating new stories for the future.

Elders can share, woven into the stories, their family values of celebrating victories together as a family. Of sticking together through thick and thin. Of supporting one another in difficult situations. Of taking courage even in the darkest days. Think of the encouragement this offers to younger family members when they hit their own roadblocks!

Even through the conflicts, tensions, and disputes, families are sealed with a deep and unique bond. High performance families understand the important of this bond and reinforce it by telling their family's own unique stories.

Remember these three reasons why storytelling is so vital to your family:

1. **Your family stories hold you together** through change and turmoil.

2. **Telling the family stories and keeping your family history alive helps your kids and grandkids** remember what your family is all about, where it came from, and, most important, where it is going.

3. **Stories help family members discover commonalities and shared values** and inspire them to live up to the legacy that has been handed down to them.

If you want a happy, prosperous family, tell your stories. Refine them. Tell them over and over, and make storytelling a tradition. Make sure your descendants know the stories and can tell them to their own children.

It will greatly increase your family's chance of thriving for many generations to come.

CHAPTER 6

Create Your Family Culture:
Your Children's Only Frame of Reference

Pause for a moment to think about the financial success you have achieved.

How did you do it?

It certainly wasn't by accident.

If you're like most successful people, your path to achievement was a conscious effort. You envisioned what your success would look like. You created a blueprint to get there. The decisions you made along the way had your goal in mind. And with a combination of hard work and determination, you accomplished your objective.

But many wealthy families forget that tried-and-true approach when it comes to building their family culture. Instead, they take things day by day, with no guiding principles or forethought.

I use the word "build" a lot when dealing with families because if you don't consciously create your culture with purpose and planning, its development is left up to chance. Then you aren't building something consistent with your ideals. Instead, you're hoping things turn out the way you want. That's not a recipe for success, and it's why the vast majority of wealthy families see their fortunes dissipate.

Building a Bridge to the Future

So what is family culture? It is the atmosphere – the environment – in your family. It's your family's ideals, habits, and behavior patterns.

It's what everyone feels when they're together as a family.

Creating a positive family culture – one that will bring about the unity and sense of purpose required to build and preserve your family's wealth – begins much the same way many successful businesses and careers do – by setting goals.

You can start this process by envisioning your life ten years from now. Visualize where you want to be and what you want to be doing. Maybe you want to travel the world or spend time pursuing spiritual or philanthropic endeavors.

Now, visualize where you see your children in ten years. There may be grandchildren in the picture. Undoubtedly, you want your family to be a productive, happy, healthy, and supportive unit, with its financial security and prosperity never in doubt.

Now, let your mind come back to today and your family's current circumstances. If your existing family culture does not seem to be leading to your ideal future, it's time to build a bridge between the two.

Creating Your Family Culture Is in Your Hands

An effective way to start building a strong family culture is with self-reflection. How would you describe your current family culture? Does your family culture promote the values you want your family to have? What would you like to change?

High performance families ponder these same questions. They take stock of their existing culture frequently – just to make sure they're still on track. They understand that such an approach not only strengthens family bonds and enriches each member emotionally, but it also greatly increases their chances of acting in concert to grow and preserve the family wealth for future generations.

To get a sense of someone's family culture, I sometimes ask a client to close their eyes and imagine that they are back home with their family around the dinner table. They often get tears in their eyes when they recall the anger and yelling, or the fear that Dad would explode and be verbally abusive. They never learned to express their own feelings appropriately or listen to those of others. They often associate feelings with anger, so they're afraid of all of them.

Now, as adults, they have trouble developing healthy and intimate relationships. They don't know how to talk through difficult issues at home and at work. And they don't have the emotional skills to overcome problems in order to make their families and their businesses more successful.

One family I'm consulting with now says there was only judgment and criticism in their family when they were growing up. One son felt he wasn't smart enough. Another thought that he didn't choose the right career path. The daughter felt she wasn't pretty or thin enough.

Now that the parents are gone and the siblings are trying to manage the family fortune, the children only know how to judge and criticize each other. There's no cooperation or constructive communication. As they fight among themselves, their family money is dwindling and their relationships are torn almost beyond repair.

One client said his family was private, nonconfrontational, secretive, independent, and uncommunicative. It negatively affected the friends he chose, the work he did, and the partner he married.

Another told me that her parents never touched or showed any affection at all. In fact, she believed her dad loved her more than he loved her mom. It really messed with her ability to have adult relationships.

In contrast, when I talk with adult children of successful families, they describe an environment in which family members have been encouraged and supported. Their parents knew that they would make mistakes growing up. Mistakes were treated as learning experiences to guide children toward better decision-making. Children were treated with respect and sensitivity.

One young adult told me, "I have always trusted my parents to be on my side and to be there for me and my siblings – even during the tough times." In return, she wants to join with her parents to help their family thrive.

You, too, can create close relationships within your family. When you show genuine interest in your children's lives, they will want to share with you. Spend time with them. Put aside your computer and talk with them face to face. Ask them for their thoughts and ideas. Attend their activities and participate in what they love to do. They will feel valued because you care. Be willing to meet them on their turf. And listen more than you talk. They want to know they have been heard and understood.

These simple investments will begin to build a positive family culture that will pay huge dividends over time.

The Bottom Line...

Here are two critical points to remember as you build your family culture.

Lesson #1: Your family culture has a profound influence on your children. They have no other frame of reference. Your family environment is their norm, and they are likely to replicate what they have learned when they form their own families. So ask yourself: What cultural legacy are you passing on?

Lesson #2: An open, supportive, respectful, and communicative family culture creates a sense of team and bonds family members together. It keeps everyone pulling in the same direction and makes decision-making a collective process.

Plus, your family members become part of something bigger than themselves. Conflicts decrease when family members value harmony more than fighting. The stronger your family stands together, the more difficult it is for any interference to yank it apart and the greater your chances of thriving well into the future.

Six Steps for Building a Strong Family Culture

1. **Regularly set aside time for your entire family** to meet and discuss your – and their – values and visions for the future.

2. **Include young and old members, and create a safe, non-threatening environment** for all family members to express themselves.

3. **Listen to and respect what each person has to say** and write down all ideas and thoughts.

4. **Implement your family's decisions immediately.** Nothing happens until you take action.

5. **Be patient** and keep things light.

6. **If you need assistance, consult a professional.**

If you take these steps now, you'll go a long way toward success now and for generations to come. It's never too late to start. Your family culture will become the bridge connecting your family to a future of peace and prosperity.

CHAPTER 7

Establish a Moral Foundation:
Character Counts

hat underlying element creates a cohesive, cooperative family capable of sustaining both financial and personal prosperity?

The answer is character.

Character doesn't necessarily earn you more money or ensure your financial security. And because character is subtle, it doesn't naturally boost your ego. But it is the foundation upon which successful families are built.

Broken Trust in the Family

I've been consulting with a wealthy family whose parents recently passed away. The oldest son, Jim, took over the family business. Everyone thought Jim was a great guy. But he allowed the winds of temptation to carry him away and became deeply involved in a shady business deal in which prostitutes were a part of the enticement and the payoff.

When his wife found out, she was devastated. He repulsed her. She threatened divorce.

His siblings told Jim that he should resign from his position in the family company. They were horrified that someone with such a deeply flawed character was representing them. They were disgusted because his morals so violently opposed their own. And they were fearful that his behavior would become known in their community and thus ruin their business.

Instead of pursuing honesty, integrity, and sound moral behaviors, Jim got sidetracked. He lost sleep thinking of how to cover these new tracks. He became exhausted, anxious, and depressed.

Jim is clawing his way out of the hole he dug within his family. You can imagine how tenuous his relationships are. But he can't go backward and undo what he has done. He's now working hard to repair that trust and rid himself of the character defects that nearly destroyed him, his family, and the family business.

Oriental Rugs and Antique Purses

Not all character flaws are as dramatic as Jim's. Sometimes lack of character can be as simple as lying when you're afraid to tell the truth. You convince yourself that bending the truth, just this once, won't really matter.

But bending the truth is a slippery slope that leads to dishonesty creeping into other areas of your life. It makes you untrustworthy, which damages both personal and business relationships.

Recently I worked with a family trying to divide the household items in the family home after the last parent passed away. It was a large estate home with many antiques and museum-quality valuables. One brother kept slipping into the warehouse and snatching oriental rugs, antique purses, beautifully framed photographs of ancestors, and family documents dating back 200 years.

When the sisters questioned their brother about the missing items, he simply said he didn't know what had happened to them. They knew he had taken them, but there was nothing they could do. The trust between them vanished and will likely never be rebuilt.

The sisters were angry at the loss of these sentimental and valuable articles. But most of all, they were disappointed in their brother, a man they had loved for many years who had degenerated into a person of low character. The loss of the brother they knew far outweighed the loss of the valuables.

Are You a Moral Compass?

If you're a parent or a grandparent, there's an additional purpose of constantly monitoring your character – of making sure you are living an upstanding life. You are the most important role model your kids will ever have, and they imitate your behavior far more than your words.

Even when your kids become adults, they still look to you to be the moral compass in their lives. They watch how you behave and how you treat other people. They take their cues from you.

I met Natasha when she was twenty one. Her mother is an alcoholic and has been divorced four times, with lots of boyfriends in between. Her mother has never worked because she lives very well off of her family trusts. She's immature, selfish, self-centered, and considers only what works for her without regard for how it affects Natasha.

Natasha doesn't want to live like her mother. She doesn't want to become an alcoholic. But she has watched her mom slug a few drinks every time discomfort or anxiety spilled into her life, and Natasha fights against the urge to do the same.

Natasha is now in a serious relationship that resembles her mother's marriages. But it's difficult for Natasha to change because her mother is still the most important adult in her life. Her mother is her role model – character flaws and all.

Natasha wants to have a job that pays for her lifestyle, even though she also receives monthly checks from her family trust. But she doesn't know how to talk with her mother about career possibilities because her mom doesn't understand. Natasha is fighting against her mother's character and trying to build a better life for herself. But her mother's behavior has made that an uphill battle.

Like Red Wine on a Cashmere Sweater...

My two daughters each have a two-year-old. They tease me because both toddlers repeat my phrases from time to time. One has picked up, "Oh, honestly!" The other uses, "What the heck?"

It's obvious that my grandchildren pay close attention to what I say and do. How I behave in front of them leaves much the same imprint as spilling a glass of red wine on a white cashmere sweater. Once it's there, it's really hard to remove. Am I helping them build good character? Or will they have to overcome the negative influence of my behaviors?

If you place great value on materialism, your children will do the same. If you put on a show and flaunt your wealth in public, your children will probably do the same. If you cheat – on your income taxes, on your spouse, on your restaurant bill – it's like giving your children a pass to cheat as well. So don't be surprised if they get caught cheating on their SATs, copying someone else's term paper, or denying bad behavior.

Demonstrations of your character take a wide variety of forms... and kids learn to mimic them all.

The Greatest Gift of All

All is not lost. Take comfort in knowing that instilling character in your children is within your control. If you live your life with honesty and integrity, they will learn to do the same. If you are generous and thoughtful of others, they will follow suit. If you have a good work ethic and put your passion and energy into producing rather than consuming, they will value that as well.

Sometimes we get so busy dealing with the urgent things at hand – in business and at home – that we don't take time to examine the state of affairs in our families.

With that in mind, I urge you to take a deep and honest look at your behavior by following these four steps:

1. **Make a list of character traits** that are important to you and your family's success.

2. **Talk with your kids about character** and why it's important.

3. **Analyze whether or not you are living up to the character traits you deem valuable.**

4. **Take specific steps** to align your daily behavior with your ideals.

I recommend that you periodically call "time out" in life to assess where your family is and where you want it to be. These moments help remind you of the long-term goals that can sometimes get lost in the noise of your everyday routines. They also reinforce a sense of mission and purpose in your life.

We all want happiness and well-being for our loved ones. One of the best ways to accomplish that is to act as a shining example of high character in words and deeds. Be the person you want your children to be. It won't always be easy... but it may be the greatest gift you can give them.

CHAPTER 8

Set the Stage for Honesty:
The Backbone of a Successful Family

My daughter Carol taught me a good lesson some years ago...

During her senior year in high school she went to a keg party with some friends. Carol drank too much beer. She tripped over the keg... and broke her nose.

She didn't confess to me that night. But in the morning she woke up with two black eyes, a sore nose, and a defeated spirit. She came forth with the entire story – no details omitted.

I disapproved of her behavior. But I contained myself and listened calmly to her story.

Carol had to have surgery and wear a drip pad under her nose for several days. She couldn't play in the spring soccer season. She had to miss a spring break camping trip with her friends.

The universe punished her more than I ever could have. So I used the opportunity to talk to her about the consequences of drinking. And I told her that I appreciated her honesty.

Her friends knew exactly what had happened. But no one ever mentioned a word of it to me. Carol could have lied. She could have made up a different story about how she broke her nose. But she decided to take the high road and be honest.

Years later, I asked Carol why she had chosen to tell the truth. She said that I had already proven that I would not humiliate her or be unreasonable. She was happy to get it off her chest and be relieved of her guilt.

The Backbone of a Successful Family

When my daughters were young I told them that I would always go out on a limb to support them, defend them... even fight for them. But if I found out that they had lied to me, it would change the nature of our relationship. Once that trust was broken, it would take a long time to build it back.

It's the same in any relationship. When you can't count on your spouse to be open and honest with you, a wedge of doubt and suspicion grows between you. When you experience a colleague, friend, or business partner not coming clean, it throws a dark shadow on your interactions with them. Honesty builds trust and respect. Without it, your relationships suffer. Your family suffers.

Character development can get lost in the everyday frenzy of life. Because you're so busy, it's easy to miss the important family components that create solidarity and success in a family. But it's important to take time out. Slow yourself down to think about what's really important for your family and for your children. Put the brakes on long enough to consider, "What is the most important characteristic I want my kids to develop?"

For me, that characteristic is honesty.

Honesty is the backbone of successful children and successful families. But it doesn't develop automatically. Parents have to teach honesty to their children. And like so many other characteristics your kids develop, they learn by imitating you.

I've been working with a forty-five-year-old client named Tim. Tim is married with two kids and is the CEO of a successful family business. Tim was telling his wife that he'd been working late. But what he neglected to tell her was that he was meeting up with friends for drinks after he left the office. She caught him in his lies. His dishonest behavior has done great harm to their relationship.

Tim told me that he learned his behavior patterns from his parents. They kept secrets – in their business and in their family. His parents didn't like conflict. So they sidestepped problematic issues, manipulated facts and dodged the difficult conversations needed to resolve problems. They avoided, shut down, and withheld. Tim learned well. Now his avoiding and withholding has damaged his marriage.

If you help your children learn to tell the truth when they're young, it helps to develop the character trait of honesty for a lifetime. If you model dishonesty for your children, it will promote dishonesty into adulthood.

Setting the Stage for Honesty

You want your children to be honest. You don't want them to cheat, lie, or steal. But what's the best way to teach them?

You might believe it's your job to punish dishonesty to prevent it from happening again. But that approach can actually set your kids up to lie.

If you're harsh and punitive, your children will be afraid to tell you the truth. If you make it safe for them, they will be honest. Kids want to come clean. But you must realize that it takes courage to do so – at any age. Your job is to set the stage and create the environment in which they can be brave enough to be honest.

At some point your family will face the conflict and complications that are common in affluent families. Working through your problems requires candid talks about facts and feelings. Without it, you won't be able to unravel the tangled web of issues that often destroys wealthy families.

It depends on you. Parents are the ones who have both the responsibility and the privilege of teaching their kids to be honest. Here are three steps you can take to help your kids learn:

1. **Talk with your kids about the value of honesty at an early age** – Tell them how important it is to all of you that you can always count on each other to tell the truth – even when it's difficult. If there's no honesty between parents and children, there won't be closeness or trust in your family. The best way to ward off conflict as your family grows and expands is to teach the value of honesty when your kids are young.

2. **Model honesty for your children** – You can't expect your kids to be honest with you if you're not honest with them. If they ask you an awkward question, be brief but forthright. If you lie when it's painful or embarrassing to tell the truth, don't assume your kids will blurt out the truth when it's tough for them. Everyone has the right to privacy. Sharing very personal details is inappropriate. But your goal should be to create an open environment where everyone feels comfortable being truthful.

3. **Emphasize honesty more than the punishment of dishonesty** – Lying should have consequences. But your kids need to know there's a benefit for them in being honest. If you glide over their courage in pouring out the truth and jump to a punishment, they won't be quick to fess up the next time. Be firm on honesty... but tender on your kids.

Everyone has the ability to be honest. But if you don't practice it, both you and your kids may develop the habit of cutting corners, fudging, and telling white lies – because it's easier. Honesty has to be nurtured, and you have the opportunity to help your kids develop the characteristic of being truthful. Don't lower your standards. But do understand that your children might not be perfect every time. Fortunately, perfection isn't our goal.

A family that insists on and nurtures honesty is the kind of family that can thrive for generations and leave a legacy of which family members can be proud.

CHAPTER 9

Get Comfortable Talking About Money:

The Most Dangerous Topic in Any Relationship

A female client once told me that she got her money the old-fashioned way: by divorce.

It's a funny line that reflects the traditional thinking of the man as the breadwinner in a marriage and the source of family wealth. But the truth is that times have changed.

Today, many women have more financial assets than their male partners. More young women attend college than young men. And although the glass ceiling still exists, more women are building successful businesses and excelling in high-level careers than ever before.

Plus, traditional inheritance traditions have changed. Today, parents tend to leave their daughters and their sons an equal amount of the family wealth. In these families, inherited wealth results in women having more money than their husbands.

But money and the changing dynamics of family wealth aren't easy topics to talk about in relationships. People are more reticent to talk about money than almost anything else... including their sex lives. It's a tricky and revealing topic of discussion.

The Core of Your Values

Even when families fit the traditional model – where the men earn the money and the women manage the home – money is too often never discussed among family members. It's often considered tacky to talk about money, so members of a couple don't know how each other think or what they want for the future.

I recently consulted with a family in which money was the cause of most of the conflict. Because the entrepreneur was a humble, quiet man, he didn't like to talk about his wealth. He lived a low-profile life and didn't want to acknowledge that he had made several hundred million dollars when he sold his pharmaceutical company.

After his first wife died, he married a woman who had hardly any assets. She nearly fell off her chair when the attorneys told her the net worth of her husband. Yet, they never continued the conversations.

She didn't know what was important to him about his money or what he wanted to teach his children about it. She didn't know in what ways he was proud of his accomplishments and what he regretted. He didn't tell her the stories about how he grew his company to such great heights. They never talked about what he liked to spend money on or what he objected to. He never shared his visions of how he wanted to influence the world with the financial opportunities he had.

They just didn't talk about money.

Think about how much you can learn about someone by asking them about the importance of money in their life and what purpose it serves. The answers to those questions cut to the core of a person's values.

And having those discussions is essential if you want to have a successful marriage.

A Failure to Communicate

In most marriages there is inequality between spouses in their backgrounds, experiences, and values around money and wealth. But when the woman has more money than the man, there are unique challenges.

A couple of years ago I met Marilyn and Jeff. They're a middle-aged couple with money at the root of their marital problems. Marilyn lived off a trust fund from her parents. She resented Jeff because she had more money than he earned at his job. She didn't like paying for the majority of their living expenses. Jeff felt emasculated because he wasn't earning enough to keep up with their lifestyle.

Marilyn and Jeff didn't talk about their needs, values, or how they felt. They grew distant as their problems festered. Their inability to communicate about the most relevant issue in their relationship damaged their mutual respect and their intimacy. It also deeply damaged their relationship.

Money may be the hardest topic for couples to discuss even though it's one of the most important.

Ceding Control

In my experience, some women still want to feel taken care of financially. Our society still believes that a man is financially responsible for his wife and children. But often these cultural expectations are out of sync with the achievements and positions of women – especially in the homes of the wealthy.

Women can also become dependent on their wealth for their sense of identity and their social position. Their self-esteem is grounded in their affluence rather than in their accomplishments. So they hold tightly to their money. They fear that if they lose it, their value as a person will be gone as well.

Some women still believe they can't support themselves, especially if they have inherited their wealth. So the fear of losing their money and becoming a "bag lady" results in stinginess. They are less generous in philanthropy and more tight-fisted in divorce. I once had a client who was worth more than $100 million and was married to a man with almost no assets. At the divorce, she begrudgingly left him with only a used car and a studio apartment.

But women who cede control by turning their money over to their husbands to manage aren't helping themselves either. Women need to learn how to handle their own money and make important decisions about expenditures, investments, and estate plans.

Bearing the Burden

In our culture, it's accepted that men bear the burden of bringing home the bacon. But when a man marries a woman with greater financial wealth and higher social class, the union is often looked down upon by the woman's family and society.

Husbands often feel powerless, embarrassed, judged, and controlled when their wives have more money than they do. We know intellectually that people should not be defined by their money. But our culture often gives us the opposite message.

This can be hard for men to accept. They begin to question if they're inadequate. They wonder if they're not ambitious enough. It wreaks havoc with their self-esteem, even when they have successful careers.

I once had a wealthy friend whose daughter married a man of lesser means. My friend was sensitive to the potential self-esteem issues of his son-in-law. He felt his daughter had all the power in their marriage. Often the spouse with the most money exerts the power and makes the major decisions. My friend did not want to see that dynamic ruin his daughter's marriage.

In an act of enormous generosity, my friend signed over a considerable asset to his son-in-law. But this newfound wealth led the son-in-law into a life of cocaine addiction and an eventual divorce. The son-in-law waltzed into the sunset, taking his father-in-law's money with him.

Five Steps to Make It Work

Acknowledging and discussing financial inequality and the changing dynamics of family wealth is the key to overcoming these issues. Most affluent families don't talk about money at all. So this may seem like a tall order. But it's the path to happy and healthy marriages and families.

A couple I know – Carrie and George – made it work. Carrie started a business with her first husband and her family money. When they divorced, she kept the business and soon met George, a retired social worker. Both Carrie and George recognized the potential problems if they ignored the glaring differences in their financial resources.

They began their marriage with constant communication. They shared their thoughts on money and what it meant to each of them. They had frank discussions about the balance of power between them and how they would handle decision-making. They spoke honestly about their working relationship and their titles within the company.

The result? They became successful business partners and intimate marital partners. Twenty-five years later they sold their company for $80 million and continue to respect and enjoy each other today.

George and Carrie's behavior is the same as that of other wealthy couples I've encountered who have forged successful marriages by acknowledging financial differences and communicating about money instead of choosing the destructive path of denial.

From those experiences I have come up with five steps you can take to talk about money in a healthy and productive way in your marriage.

1. **Share your feelings and experiences** – Set aside time to talk through your thoughts about and experiences with money. Listen to each other!

2. **Uncover family values about money** – Discuss and examine your inherited values about money, power, and success in an open way.

3. **Be aware of how power is used in your relationship** – Discuss how you can make decisions in an even-handed, inclusive, and respectful way.

4. **Explore how money can add meaning to your lives** – Share what matters most to you and use your wealth to pursue your passions.

5. **Maintain a sense of humor** – Laughing and enjoying each other are the best ways to maintain a healthy relationship.

Money should not be a taboo topic in your marriage or your family. Don't be afraid to get some advice about the best way to conduct dynamic and beneficial conversations with your spouse and your children. Push yourself to get comfortable talking about money because everyone in your family is affected by it.

Your attitudes about money and wealth are absorbed by your family members whether you openly talk about it or not. So bring it out into the open. Make it a fruitful subject for discussion that becomes a vehicle to examine and teach important family values.

Trust and Communication:
The Third Building Block of
High Performance Families

Trust is not cerebral or intellectual. It lives in your gut. Trust allows you the freedom to share openly and communicate not only facts but also opinions, beliefs, and emotions. When trust is high and communication skills are good, family members feel closely connected and come together easily to enjoy one another and make good family decisions. They have a very high potential for prosperity in every aspect of their lives because high trust and good communication are keys to success.

But when trust and communication erode, families are headed for trouble. Relationships break apart. Loyalties splinter. The damage can destroy a family.

Lack of trust and poor communication skills are the primary reasons families fall apart. These are the two issues I work with most in consulting with affluent families – helping them to clear out misunderstandings, express themselves in non-threatening ways, listen without preconceived notions, negotiate differences, and repair broken relationships. The work is difficult but necessary for families to survive.

When family members miscommunicate, withhold information, and keep secrets, suspicion takes over and distrust creeps in. When they don't have the skills to talk about problems, false assumptions cloud the conversations and cause conflict. More distrust sneaks in.

Family members become uncooperative – even hostile – because distrust is poison in a family. The result is that money and happiness are lost. It's an unfortunate but predictable pattern.

The strategy for rebuilding trust is to talk. But most people have never learned or practiced the skills of communicating effectively when emotions run high, perspectives differ, and significant issues are on the table. When there's tension, they often let feelings take over, allowing the discussion to become heated and irrational. Fearing they will lose what matters to them, they come out fighting and ruin the possibility of a positive outcome. When they try to talk about uncomfortable topics, they fall into communication patterns that do more harm than good. Family relationships suffer when these important conversations get botched.

Even though families struggle with problems of trust and communication, they often do not address those problems directly. Family members allow the issues to fester and grow bigger, all the while jeopardizing the well-being of the entire family system.

Healing begins when conversations are sensitive, understanding, and respectful. When family members speak directly and listen carefully. The hallmark of high performance families is that they learn how to communicate successfully so they can solve the problems that will maintain high levels of trust and strong relationships within the family.

CHAPTER 10

Rebuild Trust:
Families Are Worth Fighting For

Trust is the basis for all positive relationships: with your spouse, your kids, your friends, your business colleagues, your doctor, your lawyer. Within your family, trust is also the most powerful motivator of behavior.

Think of it as the thermometer of the health of your family system. When trust levels are high, your family can achieve great things. When trust levels are low, your family will be dysfunctional and unhappy. A family fortune can't last in such an environment.

How can you tell if trust levels are low in your family? Family members begin to tighten up. They withhold information. They become suspicious. When trust levels get critically low, they hire attorneys and require contracts, which include every possible detail. This further erodes trust. And leads your family further from its goals of preserving wealth and family harmony over the long term.

Distrust immobilizes and destroys families. But few families address distrust directly. As fear mounts, individuals crouch low and withdraw... or they become defensive and lash out. Not knowing what else to do, they just hope that, somehow, the problem will go away.

But instead, it continues its erosion of family harmony... until a major family rupture occurs. By that stage, it's probably too late. A family legacy can't last without a unified family. Money won't help. Nor will all the lawyers money can buy.

Be warned: Distrust is cunning. It can sneak in gradually, taking its toll slowly but surely until it is too late to rebuild relationships. Don't let it corrode your family.

And the Gulf Grows Wider

For Jason and Meghan, two adult siblings, distrust inched its way into their family through a series of misunderstandings and misinterpretations over the course of many years. Now they are trapped in a cycle of distrust. Their relationship with each other is frozen.

It has taken an overwhelming emotional toll on both of them – not only because they remember happier times together as a family but also because their spouses have been dragged into the conflict. And their kids have no relationships with cousins, aunts, and uncles.

Jason and Meghan said things that were hurtful to each other. As is common, that hurt was expressed as anger. Because the anger felt too intimidating and too frightening, they decided to avoid each other for fear of being hurt even further.

But this robbed them of the opportunity to remain connected. Without continued and repeated interactions, there is no way to overturn past experiences, correct faulty thinking, and develop a deeper understanding of the other person. Staying connected as a family is everything.

Jason and Meghan sent a few emails to each other. But each sibling read between the lines and came up with a story that was not true, either to the facts or to the intentions of the other. They engaged attorneys to settle the business matters. They hoped that once the business decisions had been made they could return to a more cordial relationship.

But the business decisions did not settle their strained relationship. Jason felt even more deceived, believing Meghan had tried to cheat him in matters of his inheritance. Meghan felt her decisions had been made in the best interest of the estate and felt Jason was maligning her for no reason.

The gulf between them magnified. The distrust intensified. The emotional pain increased. And family unity became a distant memory.

Don't Cut Yourself Off

It's a sad story when distrust breaks a family apart. Once distrust gets embedded in the family system, it's difficult to build it back because the natural tendency for most people is to cut themselves off from those they distrust. We close down, avoid, and move away from anyone who, we believe, will cause us pain or discomfort.

Mutual distrust builds mutual defensiveness, which increases suspicions, doubts, and more distrust. It becomes a vicious cycle.

It's easy to point a fault-finding finger at the other party. But repair is possible only if both parties are willing to put up the mirror in front of their own actions and take responsibility for their own behaviors.

To allow the healing to begin, shift your focus from your story to the other person's story. Make the effort to see things from the other person's perspective. Become willing to make the first move and the first apology. Defensiveness perpetuates distrust, but vulnerability begins to untangle the knots and slowly rebuild trust.

One Family's Journey

Distrust can simmer for a long time. Then, as a result of one dramatic event, it can crash in on a family like a thunderbolt. Ben had become addicted to pain medications he was taking to treat a chronic medical condition. One evening at a family get-together he added a few martinis to the mix and had a car accident on his way home. When the police discovered prescription drugs in his system as well as alcohol, they included that in their report.

One week later, Child Protective Services knocked on Ben's door to probe into the safety of his five-year-old daughter. They suspected she was living in the home of a potential drug addict who drove under the influence.

The threat of having your child taken from you is horrifying for any parent. But because Ben and his wife, Lisa, already had a strained relationship with Ben's family, they saw the incident through the murky lens of suspicion and distrust. They immediately jumped to the conclusion that someone in the family had reported the incident to Child Protective Services to force Ben to take a more serious look at his prescription drug use. Ben and Lisa were furious at his family for what they considered to be betrayal at the deepest level.

When the family finally came together, the other family members stayed in their seats and listened to Ben and Lisa, having committed to hearing them out and trying to understand where this profound sense of distrust might have come from. Rather than reacting to Ben and Lisa's pain, hurt, and anger, the family communicated calmly and with empathy. As a result, they learned about a series of past experiences that had begun to destroy trust several years before.

Ben's family explained, but they did not become defensive. It was only after a great deal of coaching, and repeated sessions in which Ben felt heard, that he was finally able to look at himself and take responsibility for his drinking, as well as his car accident. It was Ben's willingness to be accountable for his own behavior that opened the way for productive conversations.

Ben, Lisa, and their family are still working on regaining trust. And they realize it will take time. It's a process. But they are making progress because they have come to believe in the good intentions on both sides.

How to Start Rebuilding Trust

Here are some things you can do to help rebuild lost trust. Not every family will have trust issues. But my experience working with wealthy families is that such issues are common. If you believe you have trust issues in your family, the following will give you the best chance of recovering from a breakdown of trust.

- **Remain connected** – Resist the urge to leave or avoid interactions with the other person even though staying means enduring discomfort.

- **Be willing to be vulnerable** – When you let down your defenses and let go of blame, it's much easier for the other person to see the sincerity within you.

- **Take responsibility** – Own your actions and behaviors. Ask yourself, "What is my part in this?"

- **Listen, listen, listen** – Your goal is to understand the perspective of the other person.

- **Don't overreact based on past experiences** – Instead, give the other person the opportunity to create new experiences and to begin new habits of communication and behavior.

- **Take your time** – Although trust can be destroyed in an instant, it takes a great effort to build it back up.

- **Get the help of a skilled professional** – It is almost impossible to work through the difficult issues without the sensitive guidance of an experienced consultant, facilitator, or therapist.

Trust is an important basis for preserving families – financially and personally. But when distrust creeps in, there are really only two options: end the relationships or build them back up one brick at a time.

Walking away from family relationships may seem like the easier option when suspicion, doubt, betrayal, and conflict reign. But families are worth fighting for. A strong family is essential, not only for preserving wealth but also for providing a sense of safety and support, emotional survival, and enduring personal happiness.

CHAPTER 11

Communicate Effectively:
Just Say What You Mean

Without effective family communication, your chances of keeping your family – and your family wealth – together are close to zero.

I've seen scores of families torn apart as a result of broken lines of communication. All family breakdowns are tragic and heartbreaking. Make sure your family doesn't fall victim to the same fate.

Effective communication is an art. You're effective in your communication only when you articulate exactly what you mean so that the other person hears – *and understands* – exactly what you said. It doesn't matter how eloquently you express yourself... if the listener doesn't understand you.

If this doesn't happen, the listener – a spouse, a sibling, a child, a child's spouse – will make false assumptions. He will hear what he *wants* to hear. He will add meaning based on what he knows about you from the past. Conflict will follow. It always does when communication fails.

I Want a Cup of Coffee

Let me give you an example...

Many years ago, my husband and I took a road trip into Montana. Since there are not a lot of Four Seasons Hotels on those "Big Sky" highways, we stayed in roadside motels. One morning, as we set out on our day's journey, I said, "I wonder if there is a place to get a cup of coffee along the way." That was code for "I want a cup of coffee." I was confused when we zipped right past a coffee shop a couple of minutes later. So I said, "Would you like a cup of coffee?" Even though he said no, I expected my husband to automatically interpret that I wanted one and come to a screeching halt in front of the next sign for coffee. But he didn't. By now I was getting irritated and fumed, "Why won't you stop so I can get a cup of coffee?" And he responded, "Oh, I didn't know you wanted coffee. Why didn't you just say so?"

Being a woman, I still think it was ridiculous that he couldn't figure out what I was really saying. But I have to admit to the offense of poor communication. I encoded my message and then expected my husband to decode it.

We do it all the time – especially with family members. ("If you loved me, you would know what I want." "If you really cared, you would know what I need.") Then we blame the other person for not understanding what we meant to say.

Of course, the listener has some responsibility too. If you want to be an effective communicator, you need to learn to read between the lines. Don't assume you know what the speaker meant. Words have many shades of meaning. So slow down. Ask the speaker if you understand correctly what he is trying to say. This saves a lot of time, anger and disappointment later.

Hearing What You Want to Hear

Let me give you another example...

A father and son were working together in the family business. The father wanted his son to take over one day and was testing him out to see how responsible and trustworthy he was. So he gave him a project with a deadline. The son was eager to perform – not only for his father, but also for others in the firm – and he readily accepted the assignment.

But about a month before the deadline, he received new specifications from his father that required a redesign. He said, "This really throws a wrench in the works. We're going to have to work like gangbusters to get this done." This was code for "I don't think I can meet the deadline." But the son was afraid to say this because he didn't want to disappoint his dad. So he encoded the message instead.

His father heard what he wanted to hear. So he didn't bother to find out whether his son had everything he needed – extra time, resources, people, support – to get the job done. He wanted to assume that the deadline was not in jeopardy, and he told himself, *My son is working hard like I did when I was growing our business. I'm proud of him.*

Another week went by, and the son had not made sufficient progress to be able to meet the deadline. But instead of saying what he meant, he gave another encoded message to his father: "This thing is keeping me up nights trying to figure out how to get all the moving parts together." And again, Dad decoded this statement to mean, "It will be tough, but we'll meet the deadline." And he said to himself, *My son is putting everything he's got into this project, as I hoped he would.*

Then came the day of reckoning. On the due date, the project was two weeks from being completed. Dad blew up. The son defended himself by saying he had said all along that they couldn't make the deadline. Dad snapped back, "What? You never said you weren't going to make the deadline. I've got distributions set up. We're ready to go and no product. I'm so disappointed in you. I knew I shouldn't have trusted you. You've just never learned to take responsibility."

It Takes Courage

Instead of a problem with a product, father and son now have a problem with their relationship. And this causes far more damage – to the family business and to the family – than a mere missed deadline.

The son didn't communicate what he needed to say to his father. He didn't say what he wanted to say. In the end, it hurt him. Dad didn't make sure he understood what his son was saying between the lines. He could have said, "Let me see if I'm hearing you right. You're working really hard. But are you still going to meet the deadline? Do you need help? What can I do to support you? How can we make this work?"

Most likely, Dad would have developed even more trust in his son if the son had kept him abreast of how things were really going. They could have built mutual respect over this project. Instead, the result was a huge conflict that caused hurt, distrust, resentment, frustration, and an inability to even talk rationally about the situation.

Sometimes it takes courage to say what you really mean. You may even be afraid to ask for what you want – especially when dealing with a family member such as a parent. Let's face it. Sometimes we don't like to admit that we need help or support. So we beat around the bush, hoping the other person will pick up on our meaning without our having to come out and say it directly.

If you want good communication, the speaker *and* the listener need to avoid making assumptions or reading between the lines of what's said. So practice this: When you say something, say it as directly as possible. When you listen to someone, take the time to confirm what he is really trying to say.

It takes time to communicate effectively. We need to learn to slow it down. We're used to getting a lot said and done in a short time in the name of efficiency. But rushed communication *almost always* has the opposite effect. And all too often it leads to costly and painful family conflicts – which we must always strive to avoid if we want to keep our families together over the long term.

Here are the steps you can take to become an effective communicator:

1. **Be articulate:** Make sure the person hears and understands exactly what you say.

2. **Have courage:** Say what you really mean.

3. **Listen:** Confirm what the other person is really trying to say.

4. **Take your time:** Slow it down and don't rush to a useless conclusion.

As for me, I want a cup of coffee. How about you?

CHAPTER 12

Practice Listening:
The Key to Understanding

The tension in the room was palpable...

The members of the Olander family sat in a circle of chairs. All except the oldest son, Adam. He was conspicuously absent.

The family members and I were gathered because there were problems in the family business... and they were spilling over into the family's personal relationships.

Charlie, the father, had inherited a small, deteriorating manufacturing company from his father. He had spent the previous 40 years rebuilding the business into a big success.

Three of Charlie's four adult children worked in the business and were deeply committed to its growth. The problem was Adam...

Although he was to become president of the company when Charlie retired, Adam's behavior was detrimental to the company. He was irresponsible. He had an explosive temper. He yelled at employees. And sometimes he didn't even show up for work.

Adam's siblings feared that his behavior would cause the business to crumble when he took over – leaving them with nothing after their dad was gone.

Too Much Control Takes a Toll

Charlie's children hoped to begin a constructive dialogue with him about the negative effect Adam was having on the family and the business.

But as they started to talk, it became clear that Charlie was not a good listener. He interrupted often. He steered the conversation back to his own agenda. And he clung to his preconceived notions of how things were.

Charlie was stubborn and inflexible. He was not open to other ideas or suggestions. He told his family that he didn't need their feedback about Adam. He could handle him on his own.

Why would a successful businessman like Charlie not be willing to listen to his own family on an issue so important to them?

Because Charlie is used to being in control. He likes things done his way. Like many successful entrepreneurs, he takes his own counsel. He doesn't rely on others to advise him. In business, he's usually been right. So he assumes he can handle his family affairs the same way.

But when Charlie tunes out his family members, his actions tell them that he doesn't value them or their opinions. They feel disregarded and unimportant. And now Charlie has two problems: his son Adam's behavior and the growing tension within his family.

People who are controlling, like Charlie, are usually not good listeners. They think they always know what they're doing. They don't need to hear input from others.

But serious problems can occur when parents operate using the traditional authority model – with both young and adult children. If you assume total control and allow only minimal input from your family members, relationships begin to erode. Those whose input is ignored feel disrespected and left out. This causes them to shut down. They lose incentive to participate and cooperate in family matters. And that's a major problem.

A Marriage on the Brink

Ted and Sandra are a married couple in their mid-fifties... and Sandra is at her wit's end.

"Ted never listens to me," she told me with anger and disappointment in her voice. "He isn't interested in my feelings and is very uncomfortable when I express them. He rolls his eyes. He changes the subject. Sometimes he even jokes about my feelings. And he often tells me to just get over it and not let things bother me."

Sandra has no one to talk to. She desperately wants to share things with her husband. She wants to talk to Ted about the details of her day – what made her happy and what she struggled with. Sandra craves intimacy.

But Ted thinks Sandra's conversations are petty and unimportant. He's more interested in business, finance, and politics. He's willing to talk with Sandra about what's going on with the children and factual information about their lives. But he's not into talking about feelings. He thinks speaking about them is a waste of time.

As we continued to talk, it became clear that Ted didn't know how to express his feelings. He didn't have the vocabulary. He wasn't good at opening up about his personal life or being vulnerable. His family hadn't talked about feelings when he was growing up. So he never learned how.

Ted was uncomfortable with feelings. Rather than learning how to listen to Sandra's, he tried to avoid the topic by any means possible. The result was that Sandra was about to divorce him. She was looking for someone with whom she could develop true intimacy.

Learning to listen to your spouse is one of the major criteria for a good marriage. Emotionally healthy couples become intimately familiar with each other's worlds – not only what they are doing but how they are feeling. They pay attention to the details of each other's lives because they know that's what creates closeness and wards off the danger of drifting apart.

Happy couples develop the habit of staying deeply connected. They do that by continually building the friendship that comes from listening to and respecting each other's feelings.

Almost Losing Lily

Lily became depressed in college. She managed to keep her grades up, but she gradually isolated herself from friends and dropped out of her school activities. When she and her boyfriend broke up, Lily went into a downward spiral.

Lily was close to her parents. She talked about her feelings of rejection and her fear of not finding another boyfriend. She even worried that guys were attracted to her only because of her family's wealth.

But Lily's parents were practical problem solvers who never spent time bemoaning the negative. So they gave Lily advice about finding another boyfriend and getting her life back on track. The rest they ignored.

That's because Lily's emotional problems overwhelmed them. They felt paralyzed thinking about her depression. They had no idea how to handle it. They chose not to listen to Lily's plea for help. They didn't hear the desperation in Lily's voice.

One night Lily's parents were awakened by a phone call from Lily's roommate. Lily had overdosed on pills. Fortunately, she was discovered in time. She recovered and her parents got her the help she needed.

This was a sobering time for Lily's parents. They knew Lily had been talking with them about her problems for a long time. But they had not heard their daughter. They had blocked her out because they didn't know what to do to fix her... and it almost cost Lily her life.

A Simple Solution

Many lose sight of the fact that communicating well involves more than just talking. In fact, listening is the better part of communication.

The strongest personal bonds and the collegial bonds are often formed through attentive and engaged listening. When practiced, it establishes the empathy, respect, and attentiveness that are at the core of healthy relationships.

Effective listening involves more than just registering the input of others. It means you assign value to that input. It means you try to establish a connection to it. It means you allow it to challenge your opinions. And it means you don't ignore it when it leads to something difficult that you don't want to deal with. You can't just cover your ears and hope problems will go away. They'll only get worse.

When family members are committed to hearing each other with respect and a sincere desire to see the situation from the other person's perspective, most of the problems you encounter can be resolved.

Follow these steps to be a better listener:

1. **Always listen before you form an opinion and speak.**

2. **Be attentive and engaged:** Instead of hearing what you want to hear, make sure you are understanding what the speaker is trying to tell you.

3. **Be patient and don't overreact** when you hear something you don't like.

4. **Value others' opinions:** Connect with the speaker and let their opinions challenge yours.

5. **Be sincere:** Have a genuine desire to see the situation from the other person's perspective.

Next time you find yourself in a difficult situation with a family member (or a friend or business colleague) and you don't know what to do, take the first step of just listening carefully. You'll be amazed at how much it can help and how effectively it can catapult you into being a high performance family.

CHAPTER 13

Earn the Privilege to Talk:
How and When to Confront
Your Adult Children

What would you do if your son were about to marry a woman who was a bad fit for him and your family?

That's the dilemma Ted and Marta faced. Their twenty-five-year-old son, Jake, was going to ask his girlfriend to marry him... and they didn't approve.

Sure, Jake's girlfriend was pretty, educated, and she had a good job. But the way she spoke to and interacted with Jake and his friends was troubling. And her values and long-term goals were in conflict with those of Jake's family.

Jake had always had a close relationship with his parents. But Ted and Marta had never confronted him on a sensitive issue as an adult. They were nervous about broaching the subject with him. But when Jake told them he was going to propose, Ted and Marta decided it was time to speak up.

First, they told Jake how much they loved him. They told him they would always support him – no matter what. And then they brought up their concerns.

When they were done speaking, Marta took her engagement ring off her finger and gave it to her son. She told him that if he chose to go through with his decision, his parents would stand behind him. Jake took the ring and left.

Ten long days went by before Jake reappeared at his parents' home. When he did, Jake gave his mother her ring back. He thanked his parents for their love and support. Their talk had made him think about his relationship. He had reached the same conclusion his parents had. And he was grateful for their courage and candor in speaking with him.

Here's what Ted and Marta did right when dealing with a potentially explosive situation:

- **They started by letting Jake know how much they loved him and would support him – no matter what.**

- **They separated Jake from his decision.** They expressed their love for and acceptance of their son... even though they might not agree with his eventual choice.

- **They didn't approach Jake impulsively.** They explained that they had given the subject much thought before speaking with him.

- **They spoke to Jake out of concern for him, not out of their own desires.** The focus was on Jake and his future, not on what they wanted.

- **They didn't try to control Jake.** They acknowledged that he was an adult, capable of living his own life and making his own decisions. They only provided their perspective. In the end, they said, they would respect his decision.

Dealing with In-Laws and Grandchildren

Now, let's see how Maria handled a sticky situation involving her son, Alex. For years, Maria had enjoyed a mutually respectful and loving relationship with Alex. But when he got married, his wife, Beth, became jealous of the relationship between mother and son. She began to distance herself from Maria. And she eventually stopped attending family gatherings.

After a few years, things got worse. Beth started to degrade and demean members of Maria's family to her kids. When Maria's grandchildren told her about the terrible things Beth was saying about the family, she decided to talk to her son. But when she did, Maria made a critical mistake. She focused on the behaviors of her daughter-in-law instead of expressing her concern for her grandchildren. To her son, it felt like an attack on his wife.

Maria also spoke about her hurt feelings rather than the damage such negative comments could have on small children. Instead of having a conversation about her grandchildren, Maria focused the talk on herself. By doing so, she damaged her relationship with her son. Now she walks on eggshells around him and is afraid to address difficult subjects with him.

Here are some rules of thumb to remember when dealing with in-laws and grandchildren:

- **Even though you may have earned the trust and respect of your children, you do not automatically have the same relationship with your in-laws.** Regardless of your concerns for your children and their families, it is rare for you to have earned the privilege to talk to your children about anyone except them.

- **If your kids ask for advice about their spouse or children, be careful not to sound like you're judging anyone.**

- **If you have concerns about your grandchildren, be sure to point out to your children, in a loving way, the specific negative behaviors you see.** Ask what might be causing the behavior. Leave it to the parents to draw conclusions and take action.

- **You don't have the right to tell your children how to raise their kids.** But you do have the right to set boundaries for your grandchildren's behavior in your home. If they act in ways that don't match your values, you can lovingly tell them that, in your home, that type of behavior isn't tolerated.

- **Go slowly and go gently.** There's always a chance for another conversation. But if you sever the relationship by speaking too harshly, you may never get another opportunity.

The Story of Sandy

Sandy was concerned about her daughter Courtney's drinking. She was afraid Courtney would become an alcoholic. Courtney's husband was a successful businessman... and he drank even more than she did. Sandy knew the end result of excessive drinking. And she was concerned about its impact on her young granddaughters.

After much thought, Sandy decided to talk with her daughter. She let Courtney know that she had pondered the issue for a long time and questioned whether she had the right to talk with her. She told her how much she loved and respected her. Then Sandy described the negative behaviors Courtney exhibited due to her excessive drinking. She expressed her concern for her granddaughters growing up in that atmosphere.

Sandy was careful not to speak about Courtney's husband. Instead, she focused on her daughter with whom she had always enjoyed an open and trusting relationship.

Courtney listened to her mother quietly and carefully. Then she said, "I know, Mom. I've been drinking too much. I want to slow down before it's too late. I don't want my daughters to grow up around this."

Courtney brought up her husband's drinking. But Sandy didn't engage in that part of the conversation. Their talk ended with Sandy offering to help her daughter succeed. They talked about how Courtney could use her mom to hold her accountable and support her. Courtney quickly curtailed her drinking, and her relationship with her mom was strengthened.

Here's why Sandy's talk with her daughter was a success:

- **Sandy approached the conversation positively and lovingly.**
- **She did not label, criticize, or judge Courtney.** Labels turn people off. Criticism and judgment are conversation stoppers.
- **Sandy thought things through first.** She let Courtney know that she had weighed her concerns for some time before mentioning them.
- **Sandy's offer of support was not contingent upon Courtney doing what Sandy wanted.** Courtney knew she would never be abandoned no matter what she chose to do.
- **Sandy directed her concern toward her daughter and her grandchildren.** She did not include Courtney's husband's behavior in the discussion.

Know Your Role

You may have issues you want to discuss with your adult children. And like many parents, you're probably wondering if you have the right to bring them up. Sometimes it's difficult to walk the fine line between interference and assistance.

You don't have the right to confront adult children simply because of familial bonds. But you can *earn the privilege* of addressing difficult issues with them because of your involvement and caring throughout their life.

If you've developed strong, positive relationships with your kids, there's almost no topic that cannot be broached as long as it is focused on your concern for them (not their spouses or yourself). And your chances of success increase greatly if you approach your children with sensitivity and caring, you are not judgmental, and you realize you cannot control them.

It's difficult trying to figure out how and when you can confront your adult children. They are free to live their lives according to their own decisions. But there remains an opening for your guidance and your influence. You still play a very important role in their lives.

If you do not have mutually respectful and trusting relationships with your children, don't give up. A professional can help you restore and repair the connections in your family and teach the communication skills necessary for productive discussions. Your kids never outgrow their need for a parent who loves and supports them. And you will never outgrow the joy and enrichment they add to your life.

CHAPTER 14

Be Careful with Advice:
When Fixing Doesn't Help

Parents and engineers have at least one thing in common. They both like to find solutions. They like to fix things.

When I'm consulting with a family, it's obvious to me when parents give unwanted advice to their kids. But when I go home, I fall prey to the same temptations as most parents. I sometimes tell them what to do. Some examples from my own family will demonstrate how fixing doesn't always help.

Recently, I was sitting in my comfy leather chair in my office when my phone rang. My younger daughter, Andrea, called to express her frustration. Between raising two small children, managing a home, helping her husband with his new business, and taking graduate-level university classes, she had no time for herself.

Since her problem resonated with me, I was ready with a quick solution. I said, "You need to get away for a weekend without the kids and pamper yourself."

Her reaction was quick: "Mom, I don't want to just abandon my family on a weekend."

Immediately I knew I had given the wrong response. Strike one! But I don't give up easily, so I gave her my next best idea. "You've told me about some great art classes. Maybe you should sign up and just lose yourself for several hours a week in your painting."

She retorted, "Mom, I don't need even more things to clog up my busy day."

Strike two!

As I paused to think of another fix to her problem, she told me she had asked her husband to take time off work and stay home with her two daughters so she could have a day to herself.

It was a great idea, so I jumped to add, "You'd better get out of the house early in the morning so the girls don't bother you and divert you from your plan."

She didn't even hesitate: "I don't want to be exiled from my own home!"

Clearly that was strike three for me!

Unwanted Advice

Happily, we changed the subject and continued chatting. But a few days later, we revisited that conversation. She remembered it verbatim. She laughed as she reminded me that she had not asked me for advice, nor had she wanted it. She had already decided how she was going to handle the situation. She merely wanted to share it with me.

There are plenty of times when she still asks me for my opinions and my advice. But when I give them to her unsolicited, she told me it makes her feel stupid, incompetent, and small. I already knew that principle, but I had forgotten it when talking to my own daughter!

There are at least two reasons why an adult child feels diminished when a parent suggests a solution to a problem.

Number 1: What you see as a problem to be fixed may not be viewed that way by your adult child. Kids love to share their lives and their feelings with a trusted parent. But they don't see everything that is going on with them as a problem to be solved. They can even feel insulted when you try to fix what they don't think needs fixing. It can make them think you disapprove of them and are trying to change them.

Number 2: It's the job of your children to separate and become independent from you. And it's a lifelong job. Even though they are fully grown and living their own lives, they're still trying to prove to you that they are competent and can make good decisions on their own. When you tell them what they *should* do, what actions they *need* to take, or what behaviors they *ought* to change, these words trigger them instantly. In a nanosecond they are emotionally transported back to their childhood days when you directed everything they did. They don't like the feeling of being a child again – under your thumb and your critical eye.

Because Andrea and I have a very close relationship, I thought I had permission to give her endless suggestions on how to deal with her life. It felt good to me, but it didn't feel good to her.

I should have shown my interest by asking questions to make sure I understood. I could have let her know that I cared by expressing how difficult her dilemma was. If I had just listened more instead of telling her what to do, Andrea would have appreciated me and our conversation so much more.

Losing Faith

My husband recently had several conversations with his son Dirk about the training for his new job promotion. Dirk was overwhelmed with the amount of information he needed to learn in a short time and felt he couldn't keep up with the training. His angst was growing by the day and he had that sinking feeling of defeat. Wisely, my husband made no suggestions. Rather, he just listened to his son and made a few understanding comments in between Dirk's rants. As a result, Dirk continued to call his dad for support several days in a row.

One evening, my husband asked me to call Dirk and talk with him about his frustrations. As he had with his dad, Dirk began to explain how unfair the program was and how impossible it was to learn what was being required. Unlike my husband, I began to make suggestions, giving him reasons why this was going to work out well for him. But the more ideas I gave, the more determined Dirk was to let me know that nothing could be done to solve his problem.

I had fallen into the trap of thinking I could fix things by giving him advice about the training. But I had addressed the wrong issue. In reality, the problem wasn't that Dirk couldn't learn the information; the problem was that he had lost faith in himself. He was feeling overwhelmed and depressed. He needed support, not advice.

After I hung up with Dirk, I remembered a situation in my own life many years ago when I had just begun my doctorate. I, too, had felt overwhelmed, believing I could never do the work, write a dissertation, and finish the degree.

At the time, my two daughters were young girls and I called them from a school conference where I felt I was being bombarded with too much information and too many requirements. I lamented about how I would never be able to manage it all.

They made a comment that I clung to until I got my feet on the ground and felt confident I could succeed – a comment I have never forgotten.

"Mom, we believe in you."

That one small statement addressed my real problem, which was my loss of belief in myself. It's not uncommon. We all lose faith from time to time.

When it happens to you, you don't need someone else to tell you what to do. No one else can pick you up by your bootstraps. You have to do it for yourself. But what you do need is someone to tell you they believe in you.

After I remembered this basic principle, I texted my stepson. The text was short and simple. It said, "I know this is difficult for you. But no matter what, I believe in you."

After the training is over and we get together again, I will listen, support, and not give advice unless he asks me for it.

Lectures Don't Help

A client named Susan told me recently about a problem she was having with her parents. They didn't approve of her boyfriend because they could see how poorly he treated their daughter. Susan could see the problem herself and was working on how to break up with him. She had wanted to talk with her parents about it but didn't appreciate how they talked with her.

They didn't wait to hear Susan's thoughts about the situation. They believed that if they found a solution for her, her problem would be fixed.

So they began to give Susan advice. "You should stop seeing him. You need to tell him he cannot talk to you that way."

Their advice began to sound like a series of lectures. Instead of accepting her parents' solutions, she became angry with them and quit talking to them.

If you lecture your kids and try to tell them what to do, they get the message that you don't think they can handle things on their own. They think you don't trust them to live their own lives. It's demeaning, it's disrespectful, and it's likely to damage your relationship with your children.

Listening Is the Solution

Not long ago, my older daughter, Carol, called me about a problem she was having with a friend. It was complicated. It had a long history. It involved the betrayal of this friend. And it was hurtful to her.

When she finished pouring out her story, I was a bit stunned. I could think of nothing to say except, "Wow! I'm so sorry. I know how hard this is for you. I don't know what to do to help you."

She replied, "You already have. You listened."

This is good news for a parent who feels compelled to fix things. What a helpful insight to realize that just listening – without offering advice – is often the best solution of all.

When our kids were young we did, indeed, tell them what to do – to protect them and to teach them. But gradually, as they become adults, we must learn to let go. Their job is to separate from us, and our job is to separate from them.

Remember these three simple principles when talking with your adult children:

1. **Don't give them advice unless you're sure they want it.** Don't worry – they'll ask if they want your counsel.

2. **Let them know you believe in them.** It helps give them the strength to handle their own problems.

3. **Listen more than you talk.** If you could do nothing more for your children, listening would probably be enough.

Even when our adult children share with us their confusion, struggle, and pain, we must remember that unless they ask for advice, what they need from us most is support and encouragement. They want us to grant them the dignity and respect of allowing them to fix their own problems and make their own decisions. They want to know we are there for them and that home is a safe place for them during their challenges as well as their victories.

Parenting:
The Fourth Building Block of High Performance Families

Parenting is the hardest and most important job you'll ever have. It presents the greatest challenges, but it also brings the biggest rewards.

It would be easier if you just had to learn how to get your kids from birth to college. Then leave them on their own and you're done. But you never stop being a parent – even when they're adults with children of their own. Just when you think you've figured out how to parent a child, they become adults and you have to start again. How do you deal with their grown-up ideas and decisions? How do you handle potential tensions and problems with their spouses and your grandchildren? How do you maintain meaningful relationships as they build lives of their own?

The principles are the same when your children are adults as when they were young. (For more focus on young children, please refer to my book, *Parenting Is a Contact Sport: 8 Ways to Stay Connected to Your Kids for Life.*) They want to be treated with the dignity and respect with which you would treat an admired colleague or a best friend. Just like anyone else, they want to be talked to with courtesy, consideration, and politeness. When you're sensitive to their feelings, they will trust you to tell you about themselves and their families – even their fears and struggles. They will be much more likely to share with you if you're open with them because healthy communication is a two-way street.

Kids who grow up in affluent families face an additional layer of challenges. They have to find meaning and purpose in life when they know there is a financial cushion to support them. As they compare themselves to successful parents, they often feel that being average is tantamount to failing. They feel intense pressure to excel in order to experience a sense of worth. In school and well beyond, into their adult years, they find themselves being a target for both scorn and envy by people with less money and advantage. They have to figure out how to cope with the reality of their wealth, knowing they didn't earn it.

There's no manual to teach you how to raise your kids. No instruction book to prepare you for what will happen as they grow older. But talking is the best parenting strategy there is to deal with everything that comes up, including the tough issues of wealth and your family business.

The goal of parenting is simple: to stay closely connected with your children. But just because it's simple doesn't mean it's easy to do. It requires constant awareness and commitment to keep your eye on the target. And to remember that when the lines of communication are open, trust is high, and you and your children feel mutual respect, there is hardly anything that cannot be resolved.

High performance families work hard to maintain loving, supportive relationships in which children feel comfortable talking with parents about their lives – the tough stuff as well as the fun stuff. Parents know that the best gift they can give their kids – at any age – is a strong bond of connection.

CHAPTER 15

Instill Appropriate Values:
The Dangers of "Affluenza"

attended an interesting dinner party a few years ago...

Seated at the head of an elegantly set table for ten, the host dominated the dinner conversation with stories of his favorite subject: himself. He bragged about going to Formula One races in France. He name-dropped when talking about his celebrity neighbors in London. He went to great lengths describing all seven of his homes around the world.

And when I was leaving, he asked me my name (even though I had sat next to him the entire dinner) and then handed me a self-published book of large color pictures of himself smiling broadly beside the things he valued most: his possessions.

It came as no surprise to me when I learned that the adult children of my dinner host were troubled. They were raised by a father who showered them with gifts... but who rarely took the time to speak with them. They came to believe that happiness and meaning in life come from possessions.

And while these children continued to live a lavish lifestyle as adults, they were aimless, confused, and floundering. They suffered from a terrible disease known as "affluenza," a harmful or unbalanced relationship with material things.

The Big Lie

Our popular culture inundates us with messages that tell us the more possessions we have, the greater our happiness. But it's all a big lie. It's a false promise. It lures people in and holds them hostage to the endless pursuit of "the good life."

It keeps them striving for more "things" when they're really just looking for fulfillment in the wrong place.

But having material possessions isn't the problem. Instead, it's the value we place on all that "stuff." I have wealthy friends who own a yacht, a helicopter, and an airplane. They love to travel the world. They work hard and enjoy their things. But their possessions are not the center of their lives.

What they really enjoy are the moments spent with family and friends. That is their main focus in life. They are generous with their time and resources with their loved ones. They have talked with their children at length about money, values, and spirituality. They've built a strong family unit based on love, caring, and respect. And their kids are thriving, personally and professionally.

What your children need more than expensive gadgets, elaborate travel, or fancy cars is your love and attention. Your physical and emotional availability gives them a sense of security, a feeling that is far more important to their well-being than anything you can buy for them.

When your kids know how much you value them, they don't need to pump up their self-worth by impressing others with extrinsic things. They already feel fulfilled on the inside. But when your children don't feel nurtured at home, they turn to material resources to help fill the void.

I noticed this recently when I talked with a teenage boy who kept getting into trouble at school. He boasted to his friends about his expensive toys. He was arrogant and rude to his teachers. He had a serious attitude problem.

But in my office he was different. He bowed his head and spoke softly. He explained tearfully that he felt lonely and isolated from his parents. Sure, he enjoyed everything his parents bought for him. But what he desired more than anything was time with his dad.

The Religion of Consumerism

Some people get hooked by runaway consumerism and feel pressured and controlled by their drive for more. They often have no time or energy for what really matters most: loving family and friends, and contributing something positive to their community. They allow money, possessions, and image to become the center of their lives and neglect the relationships that could actually make them happy.

As research from psychology professor Tim Kasser of Knox College has shown, people who adopt a religion of consumerism and materialism do not become more satisfied with their lives or more emotionally healthy. Often, the reverse is true. Materialistic people experience increased unhappiness. Strong materialistic values are associated with a pervasive undermining of a sense of well-being. The result is often depression, anxiety, personality disorders, narcissism, and antisocial behavior.

Four Steps to Success

A thirty-year-old man I know constantly reminds others what kind of car he drives, the fancy places he stays on his vacations, and how much his wife spends on her clothes. I wondered why he always felt the need to do so... until I thought of his father.

His dad makes sure you know what brand of expensive watch he wears and that he flies first class. He loves to say that his wife's favorite sport is shopping. And he seems proud to admit how much of her spending ends up on his credit card. This man places value on letting people know how much money he has and how much he spends. Not surprisingly, his son has thoroughly absorbed that message.

97

Children develop their value systems in large part by imitating their parents. If you want your children to live meaningful and fulfilling lives, you must teach them healthy values regarding money and materialism. Here are four steps you can take to do that:

1. **Understand your money values** – Your money values are your emotionally backed beliefs, thoughts, and behaviors about what's important to you about money. Examine your attitudes and experiences regarding money and possessions. What do you want your children to learn about them? Are you living the values you want them to emulate? Remember, your kids learn from your behavior and the environment around them.

2. **Focus on relationship building** – People who focus on materialistic goals often do so at the expense of gratifying personal relationships. Materialistic values often crowd out more meaningful pursuits. In contrast, psychological health comes from strong, positive relationships in which children feel close and connected to their families. When your kids feel accepted and secure, they're less likely to turn to materialistic things.

   No matter what your business and social obligations are, you must make time for your kids. The greatest gift you can give your kids is not the one wrapped up with a ribbon. It's your time, love, and emotional support.

3. **Don't keep up with the Joneses** – Perhaps you've discovered that you're caught up in living an ostentatious lifestyle. Maybe your own measure of success has come to mean having more or spending more than anyone else. If so, you're fighting a losing battle. There will always be someone with more.

   I've had clients who spent $80,000 a month on clothes and accessories for just two people. And when they visited their adult children, they spent more time shopping than being with their kids. They were unhappy with themselves and each other.

True happiness comes from purposeful actions and concern for others. Take time to identify the relationships and activities that bring meaning to your life. Then structure your life around those things.

4. **Address the issue of materialism** – Kids need to be taught to value the right things. They need to know that personal fulfillment comes from kinship, kindness, and compassion, not designer clothes and fancy toys. When you talk to your kids about consumption, status, and money, it helps them become less obsessed with those things.

In one family I worked with recently, the father worked himself up from poverty to great wealth. But he never talked with his kids about money. He only created trusts to dole out huge distributions to each of them. His kids never had to work – so they didn't. Now the father is ill and his children are trying to figure out how to run his businesses. But they're woefully incompetent and irresponsible.

There's no substitute for talking with – and listening to – your kids. It creates transparency and develops trust. If you're uncomfortable addressing these topics with your kids, seek professional help. A skilled facilitator can help you structure dialogues about materialism and family values that can be remarkably beneficial.

CHAPTER 16

Deal with the Pressure:
Affluent Kids are "At Risk"

A fter my first session with Jenny and her parents, I sat in my office pondering... why?

Why would a sweet, shy fourteen-year-old try to hang herself in her bedroom closet? And why would she cut her forearms, creating scars she would cover up with long-sleeve shirts?

Sitting in a circle of chairs, Jenny's dad had barely said anything. Jenny sat quietly looking down at her hands folded in her lap. She half-heartedly protested whenever her mom said something she disagreed with. Mom did all the talking. She described her family's affluent lifestyle. She shared how involved they were in Jenny's life. She made it clear that they cared deeply about her.

But I didn't find the answers to my questions until I spoke with Jenny alone...

You see, Jenny felt like a failure – like she could do nothing right. Her mom told her how to dress, what to say to the girls in school, and who to hang out with. Mom criticized Jenny for saying things that might bring ridicule from the popular kids. She totally controlled her daughter.

Jenny hadn't wanted to kill herself that night in her bedroom closet. She only yearned for tenderness and sympathy from her parents. But even her suicide attempt backfired. Her mom only scolded her for trying such a stupid thing.

It's no wonder Jenny turned to self-destructive behavior. Inside she felt completely empty. She didn't really know who she was because she wasn't allowed to develop herself. She thought she was supposed to become the person her mom wanted her to be.

Here's a shocking fact: Adolescent suicide has quadrupled since 1950... and the biggest increase is among children who grow up in wealthy families. Studies have shown that children from affluent families are the new class of "at risk" kids.

Inordinate numbers of affluent children are suffering from addiction to alcohol and drugs, severe anxiety, and deep depression that can lead to suicide, eating disorders, and a variety of self-destructive behaviors such as cutting... and even violent crimes.

Poverty is no longer the biggest predictor of teenage problems. Such behavior is now more prevalent in affluent teens than in kids who grow up in poor inner-city neighborhoods.

So what's the cause of these problems in affluent children?

There are two main culprits: achievement pressure from parents, and isolation (or alienation) from parents.

Under Pressure

Most kids desperately want to feel acceptance and approval from their parents... and they are willing to do almost anything to get it. Andrew is a perfect example. He was doing substandard work in his English class. He knew his father would be displeased with his grade. His grandfather had donated a huge sum of money to a prestigious university. And his father expected Andrew to attend that university.

During an important exam, Andrew decided to cheat so that he would get a passing grade. When he was caught, he first denied it. Then he burst into tears and said he did it to please his dad. He wanted to get into the school his dad had chosen for him.

This kind of achievement pressure is painful and stressful for kids. To be average is tantamount to failure. They believe that if they don't excel at everything they try, they won't get the approval of their parents.

Often parents don't allow their kids to stumble and fall. They might not get into the best colleges if they have a black mark on their record. These are the parents who call the teacher to insist on a better grade. They threaten the coach with withdrawing their donation if their kid doesn't make the team. They try to smooth things over with money or favors if their child gets into trouble.

As a result, affluent children often don't get the chance to experience the consequences of their behaviors or learn from their mistakes. They grow up sheltered and protected from the real world. They don't learn the self-confidence or resilience needed to be able to bounce back from failures.

Empty Lives

"Empty" describes the way far too many affluent children feel. Many of these kids are coddled, pressured, and micromanaged so heavily that they don't get a chance to develop independence and self-worth. They end up feeling like an empty shell, trying to be what their parents want them to be. They aren't given the opportunity to discover what they want to do and who they want to be.

Affluent children also report emptiness because they feel isolated from their parents. Their houses are empty. Their dinner tables are empty. Their lives are empty.

Affluent parents are often busy. They work late. They travel out of town for business. They have social obligations. This means families often don't do things together. They don't share meals. They don't do homework together. They rarely have time for deep communication.

Kids are pawned off on nannies, babysitters, and au pairs. Of course, it's perfectly fine to have help with your children. But the responsibility of parenting a child cannot be delegated to someone else. That is the job of the mother and father.

Kids who experience isolation feel no sense of emotional closeness to or warmth from their parents. They fail to develop secure attachments to them, which causes developmental problems that carry into adulthood.

Studies show that families who eat dinner together at least five times a week have kids who use significantly less tobacco, alcohol, and marijuana. Those kids also have higher grade-point averages, less depressive symptoms, and attempt suicide less often. Something as simple as eating together as a family can go a long way toward making your children feel valued, loved, and connected to you.

The Wrong Priorities

My client Coleen is divorced from a very wealthy family. She became accustomed to a pampered lifestyle. Coleen's twelve-year-old daughter was mature for her age and beginning to rebel. She didn't like her mom and didn't obey her. Coleen had no idea why.

I asked Coleen to explain her daily routine to me. She didn't see her daughter most mornings because she was still asleep from being out late the night before. The nanny got the child up and took her to school. The nanny picked her up from school and took her to after-school activities. Then the nanny made her dinner, which the young girl ate alone in the kitchen.

Sometimes, Coleen would pop in to say hello while her daughter was eating. But usually she was making phone calls and arrangements for her evening. Coleen dressed up and went out every night. She considered it her career to find another rich husband. So going out and partying every night was her job. Unbelievably, Coleen thought she was a great mom!

But she didn't understand the link between the isolation her daughter felt and her daughter's bad behavior. Children who don't have consistent, loving attention from parents feel emotionally deprived. When they don't get the nurturing they need when they're young, they grow up with emotional problems that affect their friendships, their adult relationships, and their ability to succeed in the business world.

Five Ways to Avoid "at Risk" Kids

Money is not intrinsically bad. It does not ruin children. But it can create distractions. It can cause parents to prioritize the wrong things. And it can cause them to lose sight of how their behavior can either enhance their children's self-esteem and emotional well-being... or cause the unnecessary pressures and alienation that lead to destructive behavior.

The good news is that raising well-balanced, self-assured children is within your power. With that in mind, I have developed five principles you can follow to help your children avoid the pitfalls of being a member of the new "at risk" youth.

1. **Be there** – Make sure you are a consistent presence in your children's lives. Don't intrude. Let your kids stumble and learn the consequences of their behaviors. Don't strip them of the dignity of being able to make their own mistakes. Just always be there to support them. Remember, support is involvement on behalf of the child. Support feels encouraging and makes the child feel worthy and important. Intrusion is for the benefit of the parent. It feels invasive and unsupportive and suggests the child's only value is to please his parents.

2. **Accept your children for who they are** – Don't try to change your children to fit into a mold you prefer. Acknowledge their gifts and talents. Help develop them. But don't try to push your kids into areas you wish you could explore yourself. Above all, allow your children to find their own passions and follow their own dreams – even when you don't understand them.

3. **Devote time to your kids** – It's a fact: Kids want to spend more time with their parents... even if they don't always show it. Parents almost always overestimate the amount of time they spend with their kids. Kids usually underestimate it, indicating that they want more. Make sure you do things with your children. Eat dinner together. Play games and do activities together. Do household chores together. Or just talk to each other. Spending uninterrupted time with your children lets them know that you value them.

4. **Listen more than you talk** – Even when you don't know how to respond, listening is a beautiful gift to give to your kids. Parents usually want to find solutions to their kids' problems. But sometimes listening is the solution. Your kids can fix most of their own problems. They just need to know that someone is listening... and cares.

5. **Remove emptiness from your child's life** – Nurture your children. Fill them up – with your attention, your caring, and your time. Even adult children need to be nurtured. They need to be listened to. They need to be cared for. Parenting never ends; your job is never over. There is every reason to make the relationships with your children fulfilling for both of you.

CHAPTER 17

Set Expectations:
The Powerful Pygmalion Effect

I want to share with you a powerful secret that will help your kids reach their full potential. It doesn't involve sending them to fancy schools... or signing them up for extracurricular activities. It doesn't require helping them get high-powered internships... or sending them off overseas to learn a foreign language or to volunteer.

In fact, the secret I want to share with you doesn't take any extra time out of your life. Nor does it require any extra commitment – financial or otherwise – from you or them. If you put this secret to use, you'll go a long way toward creating happy, confident, self-motivated kids. If you fail to put this secret to use, you could inadvertently contribute to them consistently failing to reach their full potential in life.

But before I tell you what the secret is... let me tell you a story about the first time I personally experienced this secret's power.

In my first career after college, I taught German at a school in the northern suburbs of Chicago. I met Danny when he walked into my second-year class at the start of his sophomore year. The school had placed Danny into Level 2 – the second level from the bottom. This had a big impact on him. He believed the school's view of him and was resigned to being in what the other kids called "the dumb level."

But that year Danny got solid B grades. Because he was a serious student, I asked him if I could recommend that he be moved up a level for the following year. I told him he would have to work a little harder but that I was sure he could do it. He looked pleased that I believed in him and agreed.

Danny studied diligently. At the end of the school term he again scored solid B grades. Once more I talked with Danny and asked him if he would like me to recommend him for Level 4 – "the smart level" – for the following year. This time, he grinned broadly and told me he was ready to go for it.

You can probably guess the outcome of Danny's senior year. He received solid B grades. When Danny graduated, he thanked me for believing in him and for giving him the opportunity to accomplish what no one else thought he could.

The Power of Expectations

I was only twenty five at the time. I knew nothing about the power of expectations or the principles of self-fulfilling prophecies. I didn't know there were already well-respected studies showing that if a teacher genuinely believes in the high achievement of a student, he or she will rise to meet that expectation. Or that, conversely, those same studies show that if a teacher believes the student is not capable, the child will come to believe it too. He will learn slowly, as is expected of him.

In fact, research clearly shows that what another person believes about you will likely become a self-fulfilling prophecy – for better or for worse. You will outperform if someone influential in your life believes you can do it. You will underperform if that person thinks you will underperform.

In George Bernard Shaw's play *Pygmalion*, Professor Henry Higgins transformed Eliza Doolittle from a Cockney flower girl into a well-born lady. At least in speech and manners. But Higgins hardly noticed her except as an object of his experiment. He treated her rudely and never transformed his attitude about her.

Because Higgins continued to see her as a poor flower girl, Eliza never felt confident. But Freddy Eynsford-Hill saw her as the fair lady she had become. She explained to him, "I know I can be a lady to you because you always treat me as a lady and always will." People become what others believe them to be. They achieve what significant people in their lives believe they can achieve.

The Pygmalion Effect at Home

The phenomenon of the Pygmalion effect is also true in organizations. The way managers treat subordinates, and what they expect of them, largely determines their performance. It's also true of families.

What you say to your kids will either help them reach success or knock them down, deflate their self-esteem, and foster a lack of confidence. Your attitude toward them will spill into their psyche and influence how they feel about themselves.

Let me give you an example from a recent client. When Betsy's daughter Sophie was a child, she had a frustratingly slow morning routine. Although her younger sister hit the floor running, Sophie rolled out of bed and spent her first ten minutes cuddling with the dog. That put her ten minutes behind schedule. Betsy could have simply awakened Sophie ten minutes earlier to give her time to wake up. Instead, Betsy nagged her to hurry, hurry, hurry.

Betsy didn't realize it until several years later when we talked, but Sophie's behavior had created an attitude within her mom that carried over as Sophie grew older. When Sophie was in high school her mom was constantly on her case about being late for school and not meeting deadlines. Although Sophie was prone to dallying from time to time, she was responsible with her obligations. Betsy's comments were hurtful to Sophie. One day, Sophie confronted her mom: "Mom, why do you always rag on me about being late? You know I'm always on time when it matters and I get my work done when it's supposed to be done."

That was a wake-up call for Betsy. She suddenly realized that she had subconsciously developed a belief that her daughter was not productive or conscientious. Neither was true. Betsy let go of her old negative attitudes and adopted a new way of communicating. She learned to talk with Sophie in a way that let her know she believed in her – that Sophie would naturally fulfill her obligations and meet her deadlines. Betsy was grateful that she was able to change her negative messages before too much damage had been done to her daughter's self-belief.

Berating or Encouraging...

It is easy to give our kids the wrong message. We are often frazzled, too busy and not paying attention. When we get stressed, we take it out on those closest to us without realizing the harmful effect it has on them.

When your child spills her milk you might say, "Good grief! You're such a klutz. You spill your milk at least three times a week." Hearing the word "klutz," your child will believe, as you do, that she is one. She is likely to fulfill your expectation by continuing to spill her milk. Better to say, "I know how careful you can be. I know you'll do better next time."

When you overhear your teenager gossiping maliciously about another girl at school, you can reprimand her for being mean. She is likely to continue being mean. Or you can say to her, "Honey, it's not like you to talk about other kids so hurtfully. I know what a kind person you are. That's not really you." When she hears what you believe about her, she is more likely to become that person.

In college, when your son parties the night before an exam and later bemoans his poor grade, you can berate him for being a good-for-nothing and wasting his college tuition. He is likely to take you up on that. Or you can encourage him by affirming how much you believe in him and his goals for success.

It may sound counterintuitive. But there's a powerful secret to parenting that will help your kids unlock their full potential. And it will greatly strengthen your family as a result: Your kids will succeed not at the level of their capacity but at the level they *believe* their capacity to be. And you play a big role in what their belief is.

This is hugely important, because if kids were to perform at their full potential, then your job as parents would be much easier. You could sit back, relax, and watch them grow and develop without thinking too much about your participation. The pressure would be off. Unfortunately, that is not always the case.

Creating Better Stewards of Wealth

Because your children will perform based on how they *believe* they can perform, we have the ongoing responsibility of helping them shape that belief in themselves.

Even when your kids are grown and have children of their own, you need to encourage and support them. They face challenges every day. And sometimes they fail – just like you and I did at their age. They may be starting their own business... or moving into the family business. They may be going through a rough patch in their marriage. Their kids may be having a difficult time at school. It's tough out there. Your kids – and your grandkids, if you have them – need to know that someone who cares about them still believes in them.

Creating a positive Pygmalion effect for your kids will flow over to future generations as well. When your kids have self-confidence, they choose healthy relationships. They apply for better jobs. They socialize with people who are more self-motivated. Most important, they treat their kids – your grandchildren – with the same respect they have gotten from you. Overall, they are more successful in life. And your family becomes more successful as a result.

Here are some steps you can take to create a positive Pygmalion effect for your kids:

Do:

- **Set reasonable expectations for your children and believe in them.**

- **Encourage and support your children.**

- **Help them see their full potential.**

- **Support a "can do" attitude.**

- **Tell them you believe they will accomplish whatever they set out to do.**

Don't:

- Give your children false hope.

- Push them into something in which they are not talented or don't have the skills to succeed.

As you know by now, creating lasting family wealth requires a family that's capable of stewarding wealth one generation after the next. The more confident and successful your kids are, the better they'll be able to fulfill that task. And the better they'll be positioned to prepare the next generation.

CHAPTER 18

Raise Successful Kids:
Grit Makes the Difference

From the front row of the bleachers, I was watching my seven-year-old granddaughter, Kaylee, practice her gymnastics routine on the balance beam. During a difficult maneuver, she lost her balance and fell to the mat. What happened next caught my eye...

Kaylee immediately stood up, pursed her lips together tightly in a look of fierce determination, straightened her little shoulders and jumped right back up onto the beam.

Kaylee is tough. She's a committed gymnast. She practices constantly. She keeps working on each new exercise until she has mastered it. Then she moves on to more difficult ones.

This isn't the case with all children...

Kids of all ages often try things a couple of times and give up. They get frustrated and never stay with it long enough to conquer it. They move on to something else that requires less effort or that produces positive results more quickly.

What's different about Kaylee? She has grit.

The Most Reliable Predictor...

"Grit" is defined as courage and resolve. It's the tenacity you see in people who tackle challenges head on and don't give up. It's the resilience you see in those who bounce back from adversity. And most important, it's the ability to remain loyal to deep commitments over many years. This last part is especially critical to the success of your family. For it to succeed, your family members must remain committed. That's why it's so important to instill grit in your children. Groundbreaking studies by Dr. Angela Lee Duckworth of the University of Pennsylvania show that grit is the most reliable predictor of success. It is more elemental to success than natural gifts or the advantages that come with wealth. Grit correlates positively with educational achievements and career and relationship success. It's just a fact: When you sustain interest in and effort toward very long-term goals, you will gain greater success over your lifetime.

Your Children Are Watching

As I continued to watch my granddaughter Kaylee at her gymnastics practice, I couldn't help but wonder how she became so gritty at such a young age. Then I thought of her dad...

He's a professional dirt bike racer. He works out every day. He trains in all weather conditions. His passion for racing has overcome his injuries, his defeats, and his accidents. He's given up other sports in order to focus on this one. And Kaylee has been watching her dad all her life.

Who we are as parents – how we tackle problems and how we respond to difficulties – is vitally important. You have the opportunity to be a model of grit for your children... How do you act when you encounter doubt? How do you react to failure? What long-term goals have you set? What steps are you taking to achieve them? How you answer those questions will tell you a lot about the life lessons you are imparting to your children. They watch how you do things. And they continually learn from you.

The Pitfalls of Affluence

We all want our kids to become productive and self-reliant. But it's not always easy in affluent families. Money provides a financial safety net to children of wealth. So some kids think they don't have to work hard. They don't struggle to overcome obstacles because they don't have to. They give up when the going gets tough because they have the family money to cushion their fall.

One family I've worked with has two adult sons. Both sons have been given enough money so they don't have to work if they don't want to. The older son works in the family business part time, flitting from department to department. He acts like an owner. But he contributes little. His identity is tied up in his affluence and his family's reputation. He has developed very little grit.

The younger son decided he didn't want to live off his parents. He started his own business. He works long hours building his company. He's committed to making it successful and dealing with the challenges of learning his industry. Along the way, he's made mistakes. But he's remained determined to find the right formula to reach his goals. He's steady, tenacious, and gritty.

At a recent family meeting, the older brother teased his younger brother for working so hard. He told him that he was missing out on the good life by focusing so much time and energy on his business. The younger brother just smiled in response. He understood that he was the lucky one.

His inner joy and fulfillment come from what he's able to produce, not from enjoying the fruits of other people's labor.

Getting Your Kids Gritty

Grit doesn't always lead to entrepreneurship. Your child may be on the path to becoming a dedicated employee in someone else's business. Or she may become a teacher, a scientist, or an artist. Whatever her path may be, her chances of success will greatly increase if she has developed grit. Here are five things you can do to help her develop it:

1. **Be a model** – Show your kids that you are not afraid of challenges. Don't stop trying new things – both physically and intellectually. Don't quit when things get tough. Talk with your kids about your struggles... and the eventual rewards. Your kids are much

more likely to develop grit when you exhibit it in your life. You are their greatest teacher. They learn by watching you.

2. **Be your child's advocate** – Life can be harsh... even for young children. Every child needs an advocate and guide to help him navigate life. You want your child to trust you to be that advocate so that she will talk with you about her challenges and goals. Even as adults, your children will appreciate the encouragement and support you give them.

3. **Let them fail** – Kids can't learn resilience or commitment to a goal if you step in and show them how it's done before they've struggled with it themselves. Don't put your need for your children to excel before their need to learn. If you focus on the outcome (being perfect) rather than the process (searching and fumbling), you will strip them of the opportunity to develop the grit needed for their own success.

4. **Don't give too much** – You can be generous. You can give gifts. But when you give your kids enough money that they don't have to work, you do them a huge disservice and cheat them out of the greatest gift you could give them: the ability to succeed on their own. When your kids don't have to give it that extra effort in order to get what they want, why should they try? If you give them too much, they are unlikely to work for the greatest reward they can achieve – inner fulfillment.

5. **Allow for mistakes** – The greatest learning comes from making mistakes. Rather than criticizing, scorning, or punishing a mistake, use each occasion to teach your kids the value of failure. Review their decision-making process. Discuss what they could have done better. Ask them what kind of resources or guidance you can provide in the future. Then encourage them to go out and try again. Share your childhood and adult failures with your kids. This will help you build trust and openness.

CHAPTER 19

Show Parental Support:
Shrink Your Shadow

Imagine you're a fourteen-year-old boy. Your father is a successful businessman. He has made millions of dollars. He serves on the boards of several prominent companies. He has won prestigious awards. He is honored in your community.

How can you ever match up to him? You want nothing more than for your father to be proud of you. But your father's shoes are hopelessly too big for you to fill. How does this make you feel?

Take Scott, for example. His father developed and patented a breakthrough medical device. He then founded a company that sold these devices worldwide. This made him extremely wealthy by the time Scott was eighteen.

When Scott was a little boy his father worked hard but was at home most evenings and weekends. But by the time Scott reached adolescence his father was traveling extensively, building his business. And Scott felt neglected and abandoned. Not knowing how else to get his father's attention and approval, he majored in the same subject his father had majored in at college and set out to follow in his father's footsteps.

Scott was smart. But he had neither the characteristics to become an entrepreneur nor the passion for his subject matter. Nevertheless, he had an intense yearning to please his father. And he mistakenly thought his father would approve of him if he successfully replicated his father's education and business acumen.

Scott's father didn't have aspirations for Scott to follow in his foot-steps. He was happy for his son to travel his own path in life. But he was too busy to talk to Scott about such matters... too busy to tell Scott how he loved and supported him, whatever he wanted to do in life... and too busy to find out what Scott's real passion in life was.

The result? Scott is now forty and feels inferior and unaccom-plished. He resents his father's success and scorns his wealth.

The same dynamic can also play out with a daughter and her fa-ther or a daughter and her mother. All kids want the approval of their parents. But in my experience working with families, it is most common with a son and his father.

What Happens When You're "Too Busy"

It's possible you're a busy mom or dad. And as a busy mom or dad it's tempting to turn over the job of showing approval of your kids to your spouse. But this can lead to problems down the line – problems that threaten the unity of your family and your family legacy.

You can hire help to cook for your kids... to chauffeur them to swimming lessons... or to tutor them with their homework. But you can't delegate – not to the nanny, the boarding school teacher, the coach, or a friend – being involved with your kids in an intimate, consistent, and meaningful way.

That means talking with them – preferably on a daily basis – about what's happening in their lives. It means spending time with them. It means supporting them when they make mistakes rather than stand-ing on the sidelines with indifference, criticism, or judgment.

Let me give you another example. Jeff was one of four siblings in a family of great wealth and prominence. His father, John, was charm-ing and gracious in public but demanding and strict at home. He had high expectations for his kids, especially for Jeff, his oldest son.

Believing his greatest responsibilities lay outside the family, John spent little time with his children. He turned over the job of nurturing to his wife, Jane. Although Jane was gentle and caring... and although she did her best to make all four children feel loved and valued... they all suffered later in life due to the lack of support from their father.

Jeff never felt approval from his father. He was forty eight when John died. He now lives with the pain of never having heard his father say he was proud of him... that he believed in him... that he trusted him... and that he approved of him.

"Anoint" Your Kids

Psychiatrist and author Frank Pittman said the most important thing a father can do is to "anoint" his kids – telling them in words... and showing them in actions... how great he thinks they are.

Kids crave acceptance and approval from their parents – so much so that they will do almost anything to stand out, to make an impression, or to get a pat on the head. Kids who feel "un-anointed" tend to have low self-esteem and act out in a wide range of unacceptable behaviors – including addictive, abusive, and even violent behaviors.

It is not always easy to anoint your kids... even though it helps them develop healthy self-esteem. That's because it requires what I call "intentional parenting." It takes time and effort on your part. It requires sensitivity to what each of your children needs and a commitment from you to help meet those needs. Often, it calls for you to set aside your own preferences... to inconvenience yourself... and to step into their world.

A couple of years ago, I was working with a couple who had a teenage son. The father, Paul, had worked for the family business and retired early. So he had time to ski at least five days a week.

His son, Peter, was in school five days a week. So when the weekends rolled around, Peter was excited to ski with his dad. Peter loved to ski a gentler mountain because it was better suited to his intermediate skill level. But because Paul had become accustomed to people doing things his way, he insisted on skiing the more challenging mountain. And he told Peter that he could come along if he wanted. "Don't you get it?" I asked Paul. "This is not your time to show off your expertise to your son. This is a time for you to put your own ego away and bond with him. He's dying to be with you. And the message you're giving to him is that he's important to you only if he goes along with what you want."

Another dad I know finally figured it out. Henry was an intellectual and an academic. His son, Hugh, was into sports. They did not seem to have a lot in common. And the relationship between them was growing distant. Hugh loved to fish. Henry thought fishing was a waste of time. So he never asked his son about fishing... he looked askance when Hugh walked into the room with his fishing gear... and he never ate the fish Hugh brought home for dinner.

Their relationship continued to become more distant. Then it dawned on Henry. He realized it was his responsibility to make his son feel good about himself so he would want to spend time with his dad.

Henry asked his son if he could go fishing with him. Because he knew nothing about fishing, he asked for tips and techniques. They began to chat and have a great time together. Soon Henry began to appreciate the talent Hugh had developed. And Hugh began to feel valued by his father.

Fishing brought them together. It was no longer about only Henry and the wide swath he cut in his world. It was about a father and son who loved and respected each other.

Shrink Your Shadow

Your kids are aware of your life accomplishments. They may feel inferior in comparison, knowing they could never reach such high levels of achievement. The shadow you cast is big, imposing, and formidable even though you may not even be aware of it.

You may be focused on your struggle to stay on top... your failures along the way... your feelings of inadequacy... even the dumb luck that may have propelled you to the top. But your kids likely do not see it that way. To them you are larger than life. And they fade away in the shadow of your remarkable success.

To help reduce the size of your shadow and help your sons... and your daughters... grow healthy self-esteem of their own:

1. **Make sure to manage your life and your schedule so that you have time for your children** – no matter how old they are. Don't just talk about the things you're going to do with them. Do them! Actions speak louder than words.

2. **Step away from the limelight whenever you can** so your kids can see you as their mom or dad rather than as an important public figure they could never match up to. When you are elevated in the public eye, the risk of your kids feeling diminished increases.

3. **Leave room for them**, even when you are impossibly busy. How else will they feel important to you?

4. **Be on the lookout for things they do well and compliment them sincerely on their achievements** – no matter how small. You may be a big fish in the pond of your public image and triumphs. Make them a big fish in your pond.

5. **Talk with them.** Encourage them to find and develop their own passions – which may not necessarily be your own. Support their efforts and celebrate their victories. Every kid needs an advocate, and no advocate could ever be more important than a parent.

Growing up in a family of wealth has its unique challenges. One of the greatest struggles is to find self-worth and confidence in the shadow of an esteemed and prominent father or mother. As a parent, one of your most important jobs is to deal with the shadow you cast and to find the balance of enjoying your own success without overshadowing your children.

CHAPTER 20

Nurture Your Adult Children:
10 Tips to Strengthen Your Family Bonds

As Carter was packing up to leave his parents' house after a weeklong visit, Carter's mom called to him from the kitchen. "Are you sure you checked your room to make sure you didn't forget anything? You always leave something behind."

From the bedroom, Carter rolled his eyes, gave his wife a frustrated look and hollered back. "Yes, Mom! I think we've got it all."

It had been a nice visit. The grandkids loved spending time with their doting grandparents. Why did Mom have to spoil it at the end by making Carter feel like an irresponsible, forgetful child?

Mom's one simple question reminded Carter that she had always considered him forgetful, implying that she wasn't confident he could take care of himself – not even now as an adult.

She hadn't made him feel nurtured as a boy and she didn't do it when he became an adult either.

The more you nurture your adult children, the more you develop trust and reliability with them. But over time the air can get cloudy. Small problems can begin to chip away at what was once a solid foundation.

Just as in any relationship, keeping the ties with your children tight and sound requires work. It's a lifelong process.

Let me share with you ten important ways you can nurture your adult children throughout their lives and help them feel good about themselves while also strengthening the family bonds:

1. **Showing confidence** – Your children appreciate your nurturing acts as much at forty as they did at fourteen. You still have a huge impact on your kids' self-esteem, even though they may already have children of their own.

   More than anything, adult children want to know that their parents have confidence in them. The most nurturing things you can say or do are those that let your kids know you believe in them.

   Since they were young children, they've been trying to prove to you that they can handle things on their own. They want to demonstrate to you that they can make good decisions and live responsibly.

   When you question them or throw doubt on their behaviors, it doesn't come across to them as concern for their well-being. Rather, it feels like a comment about a deficit in who they are.

   Soon after Carter's visit home, I talked with him about the dynamics between him and his parents. He knew they loved him dearly. They valued family time together. They talked often on the phone and shared events of their lives. They had loaned him money to begin his own business, and they had created an estate plan that would leave their assets to him and his siblings after they passed.

   In spite of his parents' care and concern, Carter didn't feel nurtured by them. Their loving gestures were overshadowed by their subtle but constant remarks about his inadequacies. Carter conceded that these comments were never meant to hurt him. Their intentions were good. The comments came more from habit than from their desire to make a point or to change him. Yet, they always felt demeaning and belittling to Carter. Even at forty years old he still believed his parents had very little confidence in him.

2. **Giving support** – Your kids never grow too old for your support. When you let them know, verbally and in your behaviors, that you will drop what you're doing and go to them when they're in need, they know you're on their side.

   Some years ago when James was in his twenties, he went through a tough time – experiencing deep depression and emotional distress. He called home to ask his parents for help, but they were too busy to fly out to meet him where he lived. Instead, they went to a board meeting a thousand miles in the other direction. After that, James never trusted his parents to support him.

   In contrast, I will never forget my own divorce many years ago. When I called my parents to tell them my sad news, they flew to my home to spend a week with me.

   I knew how disappointed they must have been. I was the only person in their circle of family and friends to get a divorce. But they were able to separate me from my behavior. Even though they disapproved of divorce, their judgment never spilled over onto me. They continued to love me unconditionally.

   They didn't lecture me or tell me what to do. They were simply there for me. I will always remember their loving acts of kindness and support to me when I was down and out.

3. **Listening intently** – Listening is always the better part of communication. Even when your children are young, they want to know that they are heard. When they are adults, it's even more important.

   As parents you may think you know the answers for their life – how they should prepare for their career, which job they should take, what partner they should choose, whether they should buy a house, how they should conduct their lives. After all, you know them better than anyone else and you also know what's best for them. Right?

Yet, listening to their opinions is more helpful than giving advice. They feel nurtured when you listen because it is respectful. It lets them know you believe they are competent to think things through and make their own decisions. Your children are usually capable of coming up with their own answers. Sometimes they just need to verbalize their deliberations, and they appreciate an understanding and sensitive ear to hear them out.

From time to time in my psychotherapy practice I've had clients who were grieving from the death of a loved one. It was the most difficult kind of counseling for me because there was no way to fix things. I felt helpless because I couldn't say or do anything to change their situation. Often I simply listened and cried with them. At the end of the session, these clients would frequently give me a hug and thank me for helping them. Of course, I had said very little. It taught me a great lesson in the power of listening – how nurturing, how helpful, and how healing it can be.

4. **Spending time with them** – Baxter recently told me that he visits his parents every year at their summer home. He's a great tennis player, and so is his dad. But his dad rarely plays with him, preferring to play with the tennis pro at the club instead. Baxter feels hurt that it's still all about his dad – improving his game and getting the most out of his time on the court – rather than being with Baxter.

    It reminds Baxter that, even though he was a great athlete in high school, his dad only threw a football with him one time – ever. His dad was too busy to "waste" his time in the backyard with his son. Baxter didn't feel nurtured then, and he still doesn't.

    Make your time spent with your kids about *them*, not about *you*. Don't be afraid to go onto their turf, doing activities they enjoy even when you know nothing about those activities. Entering their world lets them know that their interests matter to you. It gives them the message that you respect them and really want to know who they are and what makes them tick.

Find ways to focus on each one of your adult children, being careful not to neglect one even though another requires special attention. Being ignored never makes anyone feel nurtured.

Spending time with your adult kids (one on one whenever possible) is still one of the overall best ways to tell them how much you value them and how much you just plain like them.

5. **Allowing space to fail** – At twenty five years old Katrina didn't drink or use drugs. One day she was on the ski lift with some friends who were smoking a pot. In a moment of weakness, she took a few hits and got high. She bummed a ride home with her friends at the end of the day and totally forgot she had parked her car in the lot at the bottom of the slopes.

By the next day her car had been towed to an impound lot. Katrina's mom rushed to the lot, paid the fine, and took the car home. In taking care of Katrina's problem for her, her mom totally eradicated the consequences of Katrina's behavior and robbed her of the lesson she could have learned from her mistake.

Even worse, Katrina's mom gave her a message that she didn't believe Katrina could handle her own affairs.

Helicopter parents who do everything for their kids and make sure they never fail are detrimental to their children's growth and development. It's not helpful in the long run when you write your kids' high school essays for them or demand that the coach put them on the first string.

And it's not healthy for you to bail out an adult child either.

Even if you see your son or daughter in a bad relationship, don't hasten to interfere. A client once told me that she learned more from being in an unhealthy relationship for a few months than she would have if she had read a dozen books and gone to therapy for a year. From the lessons she learned she later chose a husband who is loyal, devoted, and treats her like a queen.

This does not mean you cannot talk to your adult children. After all, that's one of the main reasons you've spent so much time throughout their lives developing and growing a strong, positive relationship. Of course, there are times when it's appropriate to share with them your concerns and your wisdom – sensitively and gently.

But you simply cannot make the decisions for them. If they make a bad choice and marry the wrong person, buy the wrong car, or follow the wrong career path, it's still your job to respect their decision and to be there to support them on the other end.

Allowing your kids to rise and fall on their own lets them know you believe they are self-reliant and capable. Be there for them. But give them the opportunity to fix their own blunders. It tells them that you can count on them to take good care of themselves.

6. **Approving of your children** – Every morning Curt met his dad for coffee before they each went into their offices on opposite sides of the building. Curt worked in the family business so he saw his dad daily.

Because of their intimate familiarity, Curt's dad believed he could say anything to Curt without thinking of the repercussions. He reprimanded Curt – even in front of others. He made subtle snide and cutting remarks, without regard for who could hear. He even told stories about Curt that embarrassed him in front of his colleagues.

Curt felt the jabs and began to resent his dad. But Curt's father was unaware of the damage his behaviors were having on his relationship with his son. They were headed for trouble unless Dad began treating Curt with more respect.

Even adult children want to feel the approval of their parents. Sadly, Curt's father didn't understand this basic principle. Instead of building up his son, Curt's dad tore him down. As the boss, he had the right to give legitimate feedback and to critique Curt's work. But it wasn't Curt's work that he found fault with. It was Curt himself. His comments were often sarcastic. They attacked his character. Rather than feeling nurtured, Curt felt denigrated.

If you humiliate your children, your future with them will be rough. Humiliation is a predictor of relationship failure.

But if you let them know how much you value them and appreciate them, your relationships will last a lifetime. They will bring joy to you and your whole family.

7. **Neutralizing triggers** – Parents and children – no matter what age – have a unique relationship. A friend, a co-worker, or even a random person on the street can make a comment to your son or daughter and it has little impact. But when *you* say it, it can cause a blowup.

That's because the comments you make are often triggers. These trigger comments remind your child of some hurt or unpleasant event from long ago in their childhood that was never dealt with and still causes pain today.

Let me give you an example from my own family. When my daughter Carol was in high school, her style was to do her homework at the last minute. Since procrastination was not *my* style, I often prodded and nagged her, giving her the message that I didn't believe she was mature enough to manage her own homework.

Now, twenty years later, if I question her about a concern I have, she admits that she sometimes overreacts. She knows my question triggers her, but her first thought is that I still don't believe in her.

It isn't true – I *do* believe in her. But that's how she feels, and it's hurtful to her.

We've talked many times about how I trigger her. We have a great relationship so our conversations are open and comfortable. They're also very important because talking is the only way I know to dissolve these triggers and allow the healing to begin.

Your children feel understood, cared for, and nurtured when you open up dialogue about things that matter to them and when you acknowledge how you have hurt them.

These conversations may be too difficult to do without professional help because triggers are deeply rooted and emotionally laden. Most of us don't automatically have the skills required to have these productive but difficult discussions on our own.

It's important to help adult children heal from old triggers. The positive result of clearing out bad feelings from the past will overflow onto their spouses and create more comfortable and harmonious relationships in your entire family system.

8. **Letting go of assumptions** – Have you ever gone to a high school reunion, bumped into the snobbiest girl in your class, and found yourself shocked at how genuinely nice and thoughtful she had become? She grew up. She matured into a different person than she had been as a teenager.

The same thing happens to your own children. Maybe they seemed lazy as a kid. Perhaps they were irresponsible or shy or mean to their siblings. That doesn't mean they are still that way as an adult.

It's easy to put your kids in a cubbyhole and assume they didn't change as they matured. By interpreting their current behaviors through lenses from their childhood, you do your kids a huge disservice.

The danger of holding on to preconceived notions of who your adult children are or what they should do in their careers freezes them in their past. Even worse, your assumptions are probably wrong.

Heidi was shy and reticent in high school. Perhaps because she was a late bloomer, her mom stepped in and took charge, telling her what to do and how to do it. Heidi didn't begin to learn who she was until she went off to college. Out from under her mom's control, she became a veritable fireball – confident, assertive, and capable.

But when she went back home, her mom still treated her like the child she had been. Needless to say, it annoyed Heidi.

Regarding your adult kids as children is demeaning, degrading, and disrespectful. And it's the opposite of nurturing.

Instead, open your eyes to who your children are becoming and celebrate the progress in the journey of their lives.

9. **Standing up for them** – Max was thirty years old before he had the courage to tell his mom he had been molested when he was a middle-schooler at summer camp. Mom barely responded.

Then Max remembered that his parents had never stood up for him when he was bullied in elementary school – or when he was singled out as a troublemaker at a high school party he hadn't even attended. They didn't protect him. They didn't fight for him. He didn't even know if they cared.

To Max it felt like betrayal.

Max realized he'd always been on his own. It was as though his parents didn't want him to rock their otherwise perfect world, so they just ignored his problems and let him deal with them on his own. He didn't feel nurtured as a child, and, as an adult, he still doesn't feel nurtured.

Lindsay's parents, on the other hand, showed great concern for their daughter when Lindsay relayed how she had been laid off from her job. They were irate because she was not treated fairly, and the grounds for her termination were sketchy.

There was nothing they could actually do. They couldn't complain to her boss. They couldn't get her job back. But because they talked with Lindsay about her unfortunate plight and showed understanding, care, and compassion for her situation, Lindsay felt that her parents were standing up for her. They let her know that they believed her story and they believed in her. It strengthened their relationship knowing that she could trust them to talk about her problems.

10. **Developing relationships with your grandchildren** – One of the most fun and rewarding parts of being in a family is having grandchildren. Most grandparents I know never had a clue that these young people would bring such delight into their lives. The bonus is that spending time with your grandchildren also nurtures your children.

My own daughters have told me that there's nothing more special for them than watching me build individual relationships with each of *their* children.

Sending your grandkids cards, emails, and texts; playing games online or in person; buying them little gifts when you come to visit; getting down on the floor and playing with them; telling them stories; making a special effort to attend their school events – every gesture you make that shows them attention endears you to them – and to their parents.

I have friends who have taken their grandchildren on safaris in Africa and dive trips in the Galápagos. They've acknowledged the expense but said they couldn't afford not to do it. I also have friends who were only able to take their grandchildren on an overnight camping trip. I suspect those grandchildren will remember the special times they had with their grandparents as much as the ones who went to Africa.

Because it's not about the destination. It's about the devotion and love that flows from the older generation to the younger, independent of the generation in between.

Your children will remember that you intentionally carved out time to be with their kids. Knowing how much you care about their children is a major gift of nurturing to them.

The Hardest Job on Earth

No one ever said it would be easy. Ironically, studies show that children make parents slightly less happy than they would otherwise be without them. Yet, parental relationships bring great happiness into the lives of children.

So your efforts are not in vain. You are appreciated for what you do with your kids.

It's a huge responsibility to raise a family and to become the matriarch and patriarch of an entire clan. Your relationships with your children spill over onto your grandchildren and affect the well-being and harmony of your entire family.

Your relationships establish the basis for your family culture and the legacy you will leave behind. How well you nurture your children has a lasting consequence far into the future.

The End Is Not in Sight

When is the job of a parent over? Never!

The job description changes, but the principles remain the same. Nurture your children no matter how young or how old they are. Continue to improve the relationships you have with them because, in the end, the relationships are all you have.

The good news is that relationships are all you ever want with them. Leave them to live their own lives, solve their own problems, discipline their own kids, make their own mistakes. You don't need to be involved in that any longer.

Remember how much you appreciated it when *your* parents stepped back and chose to let you live your own life. Your children want to be honored in the same way.

As parents of adult children, be sure to support but not interfere, get involved but don't criticize or judge, share without manipulating or controlling.

Let them *know* you're there for them – even though they may not necessarily want or need you to be there.

Your job is to encourage, to care, to enjoy, and to celebrate the most valuable thing in your life – your family. It's a job you never retire from, but it carries with it the greatest rewards you'll ever experience.

Family Governance:
The Fifth Building Block of
High Performance Families

Successful families make good decisions more often than they make bad ones. It's a simple concept.

So, focusing on effective decision-making greatly increases your family's chances of prospering long into the future.

Fundamentally, creating a strong system of family governance is based on nothing more than committing to a healthy process for making joint family decisions. When family members come together to discuss issues of importance to the family and agree to listen to one another's ideas and perspectives, they are much more likely to make decisions that benefit the family as a whole.

Businesses have a great deal of experience with systems of governance. They have learned how to organize themselves for greater productivity. They have boards and committees that make decisions about how to operate most effectively. But the concept is relatively new within families.

Even though every family governance system is tailored to meet the needs of each unique family, there is a common thread that runs throughout: a structure that promotes the inclusion of family members, transparency in family matters, and a democratic process for decision making.

A purposeful family decides to become organized in order to have a forum in which to discuss matters that affect the family. They want a vehicle through which to manage any challenges the family encounters, and an orderly procedure to help them decide how to act. This organized structure creates a more egalitarian system in which all family members have an equal vote on issues that are brought to the table. People feel respected and valued because they know their opinions matter.

Without a family governance system to hold them together, families can become disjointed and disconnected. Family members feel out of the loop because there's no efficient way to share information. Many families are shrouded in an atmosphere of secrecy, in which siblings don't know what's going on because parents make all the decisions without consulting anyone else in the family. In others, issues are ignored or shoved under the rug because there is no place or time to talk about them, and family members are afraid to bring them up. After the parents are gone, one sibling may either seize or be given authority and take over the position of power within the family.

In each of these scenarios, mistrust, misunderstandings, and misinterpretations flare up. When family members don't know what's happening, they become suspicious; when they aren't informed, they feel left out; when no one asks what they need or want, they get angry and resentful.

High performance families understand that it is their responsibility to discover their common family philosophy, purpose, and passion. They strive to keep the family together and to support individuals within the family. They utilize their family governance system to make good joint decisions that benefit the family as a whole. And they accomplish significant goals in their larger community.

CHAPTER 21

Plan a Two-Part Strategy:
Your Family Council and
Your Family Administrative Office

've been talking with a family whose personal wealth and personal lives are right on track.

Their fortune is growing and the family members get along with one another beautifully. They've thought out and executed plans for family investments, joint insurance policies, philanthropy, and education for younger generations. They've discussed rules and expectations for their next-generation kids and put policies in place to deal with potential problems that might arise as their family matures and expands.

They have a strategy – an overall philosophy that guides them in their decisions. It's not a vague philosophy or an abstract set of ideas. They've discussed each issue at great length and written down what they want for their family and how they plan to reach their goals.

They've taken the notion of developing a strategy for success very seriously. They've worked hard to build their strategy – step by step. And they meet regularly to evaluate and update each aspect of their plan as family situations shift and change.

As a result, their family is thriving.

The Umbrella

As spokesperson for this family, Jeremy, talks openly about why his family works so well together and about how he and his siblings have managed to build their family's wealth, even after his mother and father passed away.

First of all, the family members knew they needed an overall plan. They wouldn't just stumble into continued success. It would depend on thoughtful consideration of both their tangible assets and their intangible family relationships. This plan became their *family office strategy* – or their *family office*. It was the overall umbrella concept they would operate under.

They knew their family office would have to address both sides of their family – the **quantitative** side (the legal and financial side) and the **qualitative** side (the family dynamics, emotions, and personal issues).

They also knew that without a strong family, they would have no family wealth, so they decided to put as much emphasis on the people side as they would put on the portfolio side.

With this basic set of understandings, the family moved forward very intentionally to create the structures that would hold together both their family and their family wealth.

The Quantitative...

When his parents died, Jeremy and his three siblings realized they had inherited a great deal of money that they now had to manage. This money came to them in the form of investments his father had made over the course of a very successful career.

Jeremy's family had never owned a legacy business that would pass from one generation to another. They didn't manufacture widgets or own a company that provided services or sold products to the public. But their business of tending to their investments, their trusts, their tax planning, and their estate plan was a full-time job. Without someone competent at the helm, they would be at risk of losing what their father had worked so hard to earn.

So Jeremy took over the business of the family and began to manage the quantitative assets for himself and his siblings, continuing the family history of direct, active investing. They called it their *family administrative office* because the work Jeremy did for his family was similar to the work in any other office where people are hired to run a business.

Just as anyone is paid to manage a portfolio and make decisions about investments, Jeremy gets paid for his work. His training in law and his experience in finance make him an ideal person to handle the family's business. When Jeremy makes quarterly reports to his family, each sibling can see the quantitative results of Jeremy's work. The dollar signs are attached to each line item and each transaction. This is his job as head of his family's administrative office.

... And the Qualitative

Jeremy and his siblings also realized another great loss when their parents passed away. Suddenly, there was no one to captain the family ship. They felt as though they were rudderless, because their parents had guided the family with love, concern, and compassion. And now, they were gone.

The parents had made the major decisions that affected the family. They had been like benevolent dictators. They tried to treat each family member fairly. They were cognizant of the impact of their decisions on each one, and talked openly with their adult children about how and why they did what they did.

But now there was no one to take over that role. It might have fallen to one of the siblings, or one of them might have tried to assume the role of authority. But Jeremy and his siblings wisely decided to take away the possibility of jealousies, tensions, and conflicts arising among them – something that often happens when there is no structure for self-governance after the patriarch and matriarch have died.

So they decided to create their *family council*. This is a group of family members who collectively deal with the more personal, intimate issues of the family. They ensure that the family will continue to communicate openly, address family problems, discuss the values and philosophy of the family, and help bond family members together.

Whereas the family administrative office deals with their quantitative assets, the family council deals with their qualitative assets – the people in the family, the matters that affect the individuals, and the decisions that help create harmony and a positive legacy.

Matters of the Heart

Jeremy's family had always been close. He and his siblings wanted to ensure that they would keep it that way. Their family council was the forum they created in which to discuss issues that mattered to each of them. Rather than giving one person the main authority within the family, this created a more egalitarian system in which each sibling had an equal say and an equal vote.

They respect one another's voices and want to hear diverse opinions. They care deeply about their relationships and are committed to listening to each other, even when they disagree – and to not making a decision until each person feels heard.

Their family council is the place they discuss emotional issues and personal problems that arise within the family. And where they explore visions for their future and create a set of values that will carry on to their children and beyond.

These are personal matters.

They don't belong in an office, in a boardroom, or with outside people. They belong within the family – in a safe environment, where each family member can express what's on his or her mind. They are the issues that are dealt with in the family council.

The Art and the Science

Jeremy's family thinks of their family council and their family administrative office as the art and science of their family. These concepts are distinctly different, but both are needed to keep the family running smoothly.

The family administrative office is the science. It handles specific functions, such as buying real estate and making sure the taxes are done properly. It offers investment services and back office support. Jeremy's family administrative office even offers limited concierge services, such as finding a chef or arranging travel for family members.

These are services that could theoretically be "bought on the street." Jeremy's family hired him to oversee and manage these aspects of their family because he is specifically qualified for the job. But in most families, there is no family member who has the education or training to fulfill these duties, so the family hires an outside professional. Even Jeremy hires an outside professional when the need arises.

The family council is the art. It is more about the human side of the family. It's more informal and requires that family members come together to discuss and agree on a philosophy that will guide family decisions. Decisions come from the art of thoughtful and sensitive conversations, taking into consideration the principles and beliefs of the individuals involved.

For example, after Jeremy's parents passed away, the siblings were left with a very large art collection. Within their family council, they had long discussions about whether to sell it or maintain it. They also made careful decisions about how to fund education for the next generations, and how to write a policy for pre-nups to protect family assets in the event of divorce. And, when emotional issues came up, they dealt with them sensitively and with care.

These decisions are not appropriate for an outside executive. They are based on the value system of the family members who care about one another's well-being. Setting up this process requires a professional facilitator or family consultant. But once it is created and the family is trained, it is self-governing. Of course, if problems arise that lie outside their skill set, outside professional help can be brought in.

The Hand-Off

It's important that the family administrative office and the family council work together. Here's how Jeremy explains it.

Within their family council, he and his siblings decided that they wanted to maintain the family art collection because they all loved it and because it had been important to their parents. But none of them knew enough about art to be able to make wise decisions about how and where to maintain it. So they handed off their decision to their family administrative office. As head of the family administrative office, Jeremy researched art professionals and reported back to the family council on what their options would be, based on his intimate understanding of the family's financial situation.

When their family council decided they wanted to fund education for the children and grandchildren, it was again Jeremy's responsibility, in his role as family administrative office director, to research how the education could be funded, and to set up the necessary funding vehicles.

And when the family council decided they wanted to create a prenup policy, Jeremy secured the attorney to actually write the policy so that it would be current, legal, and binding.

The Brain and the Body

Working hand in hand, these two entities, the family administrative office and the family council, ensure that nothing slips through the cracks. Sometimes, initiatives begin in the family council and are passed to the family administrative office for execution. For example, one family I'm working with has asked for financial education for family members about their family business. They need training in Accounting 101 in order to learn to read their financial statements and understand their investments. That's exactly what the accountants in their family administrative office can provide for them.

When this family decided they would like to initiate a family bank, they took the idea to their family administrative office to explore the possibilities within their financial parameters. The family council made the final decisions.

In Jeremy's family, his siblings weren't sophisticated enough, or business-savvy enough, to even think of the consequences of having no family pre-nups, so the family administrative office suggested it to them for discussion and conclusions.

In either case, the family council is like the brain of the family, directing the family administrative office to do what it wants to have done. The family administrative office is more like the body, carrying out the functions it is given by family members who understand the pulse of the family best.

The Evolution

Often, a family administrative office starts small and grows as the needs of the family become more apparent. And the family council simply begins with the idea that it's important to have a forum in which to discuss family matters, matters that belong entirely within the boundaries of the family itself, respecting its unique family culture.

Jeremy had heard horror stories of other families who had fallen apart. He'd read about how many wealthy families lose their money within three generations. He and his siblings determined that they would not be one of those families.

It was easy for them to start their family administrative office – they simply hired Jeremy to head it up. But they knew they would need help creating their family council. Just as they would never decide to create their own estate plan without the expertise and direction of an expert, they also didn't want to try setting up their family council on their own. They likened it to trying to do surgery on themselves.

They realized they would not be able to see their own flaws, break through their own barriers, or resolve their own emotional problems without professional help. Because they couldn't predict feelings that would come up, or differences of opinion that might cause conflicts, they wanted an outside facilitator to help them through the bumpy spots. In Jeremy's family, as in most families, the problems that are most evident on the surface have root causes that lie hidden deep within the family dynamics, requiring professional help to discover, resolve, or manage. That's where I came in.

They began with an open mind and a great commitment to a healthy family. Over time, both their family administrative office and their family council have evolved. What they started out with is not what they have ended up with. And they're still growing.

What they have built is a solid foundation within their family to deal with most any problem that arises – in both the tangible and the intangible arenas. They have a history of engaging in difficult conversations and have come out the other side with stronger family bonds. As a family, they are beating the odds and creating prosperity for future generations.

Begin setting up your overall family office strategy by writing a paragraph on each of the following:

1. **What is your philosophy for your family** – the higher purpose that guides your decisions for your family now and for the future?

2. **What are your most valuable tangible and intangible assets?** Elaborate as fully as possible.

3. **What is your vision for your family** and what would you like your legacy to be 10 years after you're gone?

4. **What action steps are you ready to take now** to reach your goals?

CHAPTER 22

Create Your Family Council:
The Control Center of Your Family

Every organization needs a control center. Otherwise, there's no one to keep it going in the right direction, and no one knows whom to turn to when there's a problem. Every family needs a control center, too. We call it the **family council**.

Loren, CEO of his family business and father of four, recently told me, "When an issue comes up in our family business, we go to the board. When an issue comes up with the trusts, we go to the trustees. But when an issue comes up in our family, we had no one to go to – until we created our family council."

The Normal, Ordinary Issues

When Loren's parents died, he instantly noticed a seismic shift in the family. Everyone in both their business and their family had looked to them for guidance and direction. Now, there was nothing but a giant void – of wisdom and authority. Having lost the family control center, Loren felt the burden as family issues began to land on his desk at work.

This family had always gotten along well and enjoyed one another at annual family meetings. But a sudden stir of emotions began to create havoc. First came the decisions about a memorial service for the patriarch. Differences of opinion and interference from non-blood-line spouses caused resentment from grieving family members.

Next was the dilemma of one teenage grandchild whose alcohol and drug abuse was gaining attention from other family members. They were deeply concerned but didn't know what to do, or whether they should do anything, so the problem was thrown to Loren. Another grandchild wanted to do a summer internship at the family company, and Loren realized that there had never been a policy about hiring rising-generation family members. He didn't want to be left alone making that decision for his nephew.

Soon, it was time to plan for the next annual family meeting, and Loren's siblings began to rumble that these get-togethers had become irrelevant because they were never planned according to the needs or desires of the family. In the past, their parents had hired speakers for their meetings, but the ideas presented never materialized into anything beneficial for them beyond entertainment. Their parents had habitually spent exorbitant amounts of money on luxurious hotels for the event but didn't deem it necessary to spend money on child care for the younger kids. Again, the complaints now went directly to Loren.

Then it was time to disburse the personal possessions from the estate of the patriarch and matriarch. Since there was no one to determine how it should be divided equitably, a highly coveted emerald ring walked off on the finger of a girlfriend of one of the family members – who became an ex-girlfriend a couple of months later. Many family members were outraged by the loss of a family treasure because of a lack of management and oversight.

These are not unusual problems or things that come up only in troubled families. These are normal, ordinary issues. But Loren was overwhelmed and stressed out.

Going Beyond the Standard

Loren knew the "shirtsleeves to shirtsleeves in three generations" proverb and didn't want his family's business to be among the more than 90 percent that failed. He realized that, in order to preserve the business, his family would have to go beyond the standard that families normally do. He'd already read the stories about family disasters that caused the destruction of their families and their family businesses. He wanted to avoid that at all costs. He knew that in order for their family business to work, their family had to work.

So he began the process of creating a family council.

Everyone in the family realized they didn't have the expertise to develop the foundation for a successful family council or to facilitate the meetings that would establish the structure, organization, and policies that would allow it to succeed. They also knew touchy subjects were likely to come up that would require an outside professional to handle in a way that would bring the family closer together rather than split them apart. That's when Loren contacted me, and I was delighted to come on board.

A Best Practice

Just as a company has a board of directors to handle the business of the organization, families have a family council. Loren now understands why it has become a best practice for high performance families.

Their family council has become the family's system of self-governance. It is the structure by which they organize themselves and make decisions that affect the family. It has established a vehicle in which to create a larger sense of family life, to deal with specific issues within the family, and to define policies and procedures for the family at large.

As I have worked with them, their family council has developed into an organized but somewhat informal structure – agreed upon by the family but not legally binding because there is no formal legal structure and there are no attorneys involved. It is the control center for their family and it lies entirely *within* the family.

Loren says it has spread the authority and responsibility for family decisions in a more democratic way. His family has shifted from a vertical to a horizontal organizational structure.

As we have talked together, issues have come up that the family didn't even know they had. The issues had stayed hidden below the surface, and no one had had the courage to bring them into the open. It was easier to keep them shoved under the rug. Yet everyone suspected that one day they might come flooding out, spilling onto others in the family in destructive ways. With an outside facilitator, it has been relatively easy for family members to bring up unresolved issues and deal with them in the safe environment we've created.

Family members now have a place where they can talk about the problems of the past and respectfully discuss ways to avoid the mistakes of the previous generation. They can explore whether and how they will include spouses, how they will educate and prepare heirs to enter the business, how they envision their future as a family, and many other issues that affect their long-term family success.

Avoiding "Hat Creep"

Loren's family business is distinctly different from public companies. Families already have a set of values, they care more about employees, and they have a greater willingness to delay gratification for the sake of long-term goals. They have concerns about opportunities for their children, a greater sense of responsiveness to one another's needs, and a commitment to keeping promises. This sets them apart from public companies and gives them a greater advantage.

Yet, getting caught in the gray areas between family and business, as well as not dealing with unhealthy family dynamics, can rip the family apart and quickly destroy this advantage – along with the business itself.

Loren was aware of this potential problem. As we have worked together, one principle I have impressed upon them is not to allow "hat creep" – that gradual blurring of the boundaries between the family and the business, in which family members think they have a right to interfere with family business decisions.

Just as no shareholder can walk into a publicly held company and begin to dictate policy, neither can a family member walk into his or her privately held family business and begin to criticize or demand. Even gentle suggestions are often not accepted kindly by management.

The members of Loren's family council have become more sensitive about interacting appropriately with the family business. As they have learned to separate family from business, and to speak with one unified and cohesive voice, they have developed greater trust between themselves and their board and top management. It is within this environment that they are now invited to ask questions in order to educate themselves about the business so that they will be prepared to make the important decisions necessary to maintain and grow their wealth.

When family members learn to become excellent beneficiaries, when there's a good relationship between family members and those responsible for running their business, and when family members understand their roles and responsibilities, then the family can make healthy transitions at each new fork in the road. The family council is the control center where this occurs.

What the Family Council Does

Loren's family members were excited to begin creating their family council. Abstractly, they thought it sounded like a good idea, even though they didn't really understand what they would do once they got themselves organized. But as soon as they finished writing their charter, they began to list the things they wanted to accomplish:

1. **Develop the family philosophy and culture,** define the family values, write a mission statement and family constitution

2. **Promote understanding and education** of the family's businesses and enterprises

3. **Create policies and procedures** (for "who is family," succession, family members being involved in the business, how to handle spouses, how to handle divorces, deciding if pre-nups will be required, how families will help children start a business, loans, etc.)

4. **Build communication and mutual understanding**

5. **Help family members bond** and develop a sense of team and larger family identity

6. **Deal with conflicts and solve problems**

7. **Explore education opportunities**

8. **Prepare for family business ownership,** continuity, and succession

9. **Keep the family history and stories alive** and recorded for legacy purposes

10. **Create a family bank**

11. **Establish financial literacy programs**

12. **Set family meetings and develop agendas**

13. **Grow great beneficiaries**

14. **Grow great trustees**

Their family council has met face to face several times in day-long meetings. And we have met via video conferencing every other month. The most important thing that has occurred is that the entire family is coming together in a way it never has before.

As family members have explored and discussed potential and real problems, they have developed respect and caring that never existed before. Conversations are deeper and more meaningful than they ever were in the past. As one family council member expressed, "We are like a whole new family, ready to face any challenge, to grow and to prosper together."

What's the Delay?

It's common in nuclear families of the first and second generations for the patriarch and matriarch to have the authority and control over both the business and the family. Yet some forward-thinking families have already begun to develop their family council – in preparation for the future. They know their council will shift and evolve over time to fit the specific needs of the family. But they want to think through the issues *with* their children and give their kids the benefit of their wisdom and experience.

It is often the case that about one year after the passing of the matriarch and/or patriarch, the family begins to unravel. Siblings who have gotten along in the past suddenly express their complaints. As grief subsides, individual ambitions and desires take over. Confusion lurks everywhere as family members now realize that they are truly on their own. With no one in charge, family members assume and misinterpret, hoping to gain some advantage in the family business, monetarily, with family possessions, or in status and position. Jealousies and rivalries creep in without the authority of a mother or father to quell them. Distrust begins to reign.

In some form or another, this scenario is more common than not. But successful families prepare in advance. They already have the structures in place to deal with all of these potential problems – and more. They have a well-functioning family council that has had experience in governing itself, making tough decisions, developing policies, and working through conflicts. These are the families that will prosper through many generations.

To get started, please contemplate the following questions:

1. **How will your family benefit** by having a forum in which to talk about family issues?

2. **How well does your family discuss topics that are stressful or uncomfortable?** Do you work through conflicts and disagreements – or do you tend to avoid touchy subjects?

3. **What process do you use** to make joint family decisions?

4. **What obstacles to creating your family council might you have to overcome?**

CHAPTER 23

Develop Your Family Administrative Office:
The Workforce for Your Family

Thirty-five years ago in a small town in Texas, Cassie and her husband, Seth, decided to start their own business. Cassie was the daughter of a wealthy entrepreneur. Seth was an ophthalmologist who had worked in a clinic with two other doctors. Now he and Cassie decided it was time for them to start a clinic of their own.

Cassie and Seth went to Cassie's father and asked to take out a loan against her future inheritance. They submitted a business proposal, talked with the family attorney and her trustee, and secured the loan.

Over the years, they were successful and gradually opened several clinics in other towns in Texas. There were no ophthalmologists among their three children, so when it came time for Seth to retire, they decided to sell their business. But they knew they couldn't do it on their own.

They didn't know how to appraise their business, market it, find a buyer, or broker the sale. They also didn't know what to do with the money they would receive. So they found a man who had the qualifications they needed. With a law degree, a background in finance, and experience in brokering business sales, Tim seemed like just the right person.

On the Right Track

It took almost a year, but Tim found a buyer, and they sold their business for $55 million. Cassie and Seth appreciated Tim's expertise, professionalism, and loyalty. They quickly realized that they would continue to need his help in order to create the kind of retirement they had envisioned for themselves.

They were both diligent producers and had no intention of just sitting back and relaxing. In fact, they were anxious to get on with the next phase of their lives. Seth wanted to do some consulting and write a book. Cassie set her sights on starting and directing a non-profit for disadvantaged children in their community.

But first, they had to get their financial life organized and on the right track. So they hired Tim to set up their family administrative office. A family administrative office is just what it sounds like. It's a working office with personnel who work for the family to administer and manage the business of the family. Its primary job is to centralize the management of the family fortune, including financial and legal matters.

At the beginning, Cassie and Seth didn't know exactly what they wanted Tim to do. But his overall job description was to manage the family's assets. They wanted Tim to help all of them – Cassie, Seth, and their three children – assess what they held and how potential transactions would influence their aggregate estate value and the diversification of their family wealth.

Tim was the only employee of the family administrative office for quite a while. He worked full time taking care of the business that Cassie and Seth delegated to him. After several months, when the job became more clearly specified, he hired another staff member to help him. No one in the family worked at the family office. Typically, the workforce of a family administrative office is made up of professionals and semi-professionals hired by the family.

An Extra Set of Ears

Cassie and Seth knew that although they were experts in the field of ophthalmology and running eye clinics, they had very little expertise or knowledge outside of that arena. They had worked hard for the money they had earned and didn't want to lose it. They wanted to be careful and wise. They realized they would benefit from Tim's advice.

Immediately, Cassie and Seth set up trusts for their children and began to revise their estate plan. Tim oversaw the meetings with attorneys, tax planners, and wealth advisors. He provided an extra set of ears for understanding the proposals and discussed them with Cassie and Seth before they made their decisions. Together, the three of them reviewed the investments Cassie and Seth had made throughout their lifetimes and discussed re-allocations.

Since commercial real estate seemed like a viable investment at the time, Tim researched properties and brought together several deals for Cassie and Seth. Tim looked into self-publishing for Seth and advised him on how to proceed with his book project. And he helped Cassie explore the world of nonprofits, volunteer employees, and how she could begin her new line of work.

Both Cassie and Seth had long wanted to remodel their home. Finally they had the time and energy to focus on themselves instead of only their business. They asked Tim to sit in on meetings with architects and to manage the permit and construction process.

Including the Kids

As Tim proved to be invaluable to Cassie and Seth, his work expanded to include the three children. One was a teacher, one a social worker, and one a graphic designer. Two were married with three small children of their own.

Each of the children had a sizable generation-skipping trust from their grandparents. Now they had the newly created trusts from their parents. They also wanted to plan wisely for their own children and appreciated the advice and counsel of Tim.

Since the children were now part of their single-family office, Cassie and Seth paid for Tim's services for them in any way they needed him. He suggested and researched combining insurance policies when it would benefit the family as a whole. He arranged for jewelry and personal property appraisals after they all received distributions from the estate of Cassie's parents. He also advised them on buying homes and evaluating major purchases.

They met frequently as a family with Tim to keep informed about current financial issues that affected the family. Tim came to know the family members very well, but he refrained from advising them on personal or emotional family issues. He understood that those things lay outside his area of expertise.

The Scope of the Work

Tim told me that his job had expanded since he had first begun working as the head of Cassie and Seth's family administrative office. It's common that families begin with one concept of their family office and allow it to evolve over time. What they start with is rarely what they end up with.

Basically, as manager of the family administrative office, Tim does whatever the family wants him to do to assist in the financial and legal arenas.

1. **He manages their assets but does not make the investments.** Wealth advisors make the investment recommendations and transactions.

2. **He provides financial and administrative services,** including oversight and daily management of all liquid and illiquid assets. This encompasses generating monthly and quarterly statements for the businesses as well as personal financial statements. He speaks to Cassie and Seth weekly. He analyzes investment

returns. He helps with budgeting and long-term planning, does prep work for taxes, and manages banking relationships.

3. **He helps with real estate transactions and property management**, obtains loans, manages permit processes for property improvements, and manages construction and improvement projects. He even assists with vehicle purchases.

4. **He helps manage trusts by acting as a liaison or interpreter** between legal counsel and the family.

5. **He helps with short-term and long-term financial planning,** manages powers of attorney for asset management and health care, manages insurance coverage and claims, and manages legal issues.

6. **He provides staff for bookkeeping and bill-paying services and concierge services** (such as making travel reservations or catering parties). This includes making payroll and a wide range of other back-office support services.

7. **He provides education and training to family members,** as needed, in simple accounting, trusts, and other business principles to help them become more business-savvy.

Variations on the Family Administrative Office

Every family administrative office is different because every family is unique, with different needs. In some families, the patriarch and matriarch are still active in running their family business or their family investments. In others, the elders have passed away and the duties have fallen to the next generation. So the urgency of having an organized way of managing the family's financial life is more acute.

In some families, a family member is put in charge of the office if he or she has the background and experience to handle the job. But usually, an outside person is hired to head up the family administrative office. If the family or the estate is large, it may require a full-time staff with an entire office space. Other families need only a part-time person. I've worked with families who conduct much of their family office functions out of their family business, utilizing personnel who already work for the business. Others don't want to mix the two.

Sometimes, more than one family joins together to create a multi-family office in order to benefit from economies of scale, sharing infrastructure and staff costs. In this way, they can often share tax and estate planning information and perspectives on investment strategies and wealth management practices.

Some financial institutions offer family office services. Their professionals provide a wide range of wealth management and some personal services.

There is no right or wrong. The important part is to get organized so that your family is structurally solid for making important business decisions at the appropriate times.

Comparing the Family Administrative Office with the Family Council

Your overall **Family Office Strategy** requires that you create two distinctly different entities:

Family Council	CHARACTERISTICS	Family Administrative Office
Focus on intangible assets (human capital)	**Differences in focus**	Focus on tangible assets (financial capital)
Only family members	**Who is in it?**	May include professionals with expertise in finance, law, and/or business
Volunteer or elected by family (no specific expertise needed)	**How are they selected?**	Employees hired by the family
Address the people problems and relationship issues within the family and interface with the family business	**What do they do?**	Manage the financial and business aspects of the family
Family council has authority over the family administrative office	**Who has authority?**	Directed and instructed by the family council
They ARE the family	**Relationship to the family**	They work FOR the family

After they had already set up their family administrative office, Cassie and Seth contacted me to help them create their family council. They realized they had done it backward – they should have created their family council first. They were anxious to start again – this time with their entire family involved – to develop the philosophy, values, and vision that would guide their family into the future.

We talked first about the differences between a family administrative office and a family council. They would be distinctly separate entities. They understood that, although they had hired Tim to run their family administrative office, the family council would be made up of their own family members. The family council would be their authoritative branch, and decisions pertaining to the family would be made there, not by the family administrative office.

Whereas the family council would focus on the people in the family, the family administrative office would focus on the business of the family. It would take its direction from the family council.

In a well-functioning family there is a healthy interplay between the family administrative office and the family council. With open communication, transparency, and trust, individual family members can talk with family administrative office staff whenever they want, and the family council brings to them questions and requests on behalf of the entire family. From time to time, the family administrative office makes suggestions to the family council when they become aware of an issue the family is not knowledgeable about. The support and loyalty of the family administrative office is felt by all members of the family.

Ensuring Their Future

Cassie and Seth's family was fortunate to be able to create both the family council and the family administrative office while they were still alive and while everyone could benefit from the wisdom and experience of the elders in the family.

Because Cassie and Seth had developed good relationships with their children, they were able to share with them their philosophy about wealth and their vision for their family into the future. Even though they had already set up their family administrative office, the entire family now got together to discuss more specifically how they wanted it to function and what services they wanted it to provide.

Through their family council, they determined how they wanted their family administrative office to be managed, both currently and after the parents had passed away. This gave everyone in the family the security of knowing that the family would be able to weather future financial storms. Because they had built a solid foundation for their family council, they felt comfortable that they would also be able to handle emotional issues that would inevitably come up as time went on.

This family was set to become a high performance family. They didn't just talk about what they wanted in their family. They took action. They had looked ahead to the future and put in place the structures they knew would help them avoid the "shirtsleeves to shirtsleeves in three generations" proverb, grow their wealth, and maintain a high level of family harmony.

After you have created your family council, your family is ready to set up its family administrative office. In order to prepare, make a list of the following:

1. **Potential functions and services** you would like your family administrative office to provide. (This list will evolve over time.)

2. **Possible trusted professionals or family members** who could be hired to head up your family administrative office.

3. **Ideal healthy interactions** between your family council and your family administrative office.

CHAPTER 24

Ensure Your Future:
Your Family Office Strategy

The statistics are shocking.

At least 70 percent of high-net-worth families lose the ability to transfer their wealth beyond three generations. This means that, statistically, by the time your grandchildren become adults, your hard-earned money will already be gone.

With family businesses, the statistic is even higher – 90 percent of them fail by the third generation.

Even more astounding are the studies that indicate the primary cause of this failure. Of the families that fail, only 3 percent do so because of poor legal or financial planning. That means that the other 97 percent – nearly ALL – of the failure is due to other causes.

The studies show overwhelmingly that these failures have their roots in family issues. Families fall apart for a variety of reasons – interpersonal conflicts, poor planning for the future, lack of organization, poor skills for discussing important topics and making good decisions, emotional chaos, lawsuits against family members, distrust, and more. These problems all contribute to the demise of the family. And when the family falls apart, the money disappears.

That's right. First the family goes, then the wealth.

Randy, a third-generation family member, told me that his parents and grandparents had been vastly wealthy. Now, there was only about $10 million left in the family. For many people, that's still a lot of money, but Randy was appalled because, percentage-wise, his family had lost almost everything. He had plenty of tales about divorces, deaths, addictions, and myriad family dysfunctions that had torn his family apart. Still, he was horrified to find himself just another example of the "shirtsleeves to shirtsleeves in three generations" proverb.

The Failures Continue

Have you ever wondered why there is only a 3 percent failure on the financial and legal side of the equation and such astronomical failure on the family side? I certainly have! I've thought about it a lot – perhaps because families are my area of expertise.

I've looked at families from the inside out. To date, I have never encountered a family of means that did not have some kind of plan in place for their finances. They work with wealth managers, investment advisors, business and money managers, estate planners, family attorneys, and tax planners. They read and follow financial newsletters, magazines, and research reports to keep abreast of changing geopolitical news that will affect their portfolios. They attend conferences and listen to the advice of wealth strategists to ensure they are making the best investments with the best asset allocations.

In short, they surround themselves with platoons of experts to help protect, maintain, and grow their wealth.

And yet the vast majority of families fail.

The Greatest Threat

The experts they hire are competent. They're very good at what they do. They're especially effective because they work long term for these families of wealth. The professionals are continually looking out for the families they work for. They hold ongoing meetings with their clients to share new information, review portfolios and legal affairs, discuss new tax laws, analyze the market, and recommend adjustments.

Once a family finds an advisor or a firm they trust, they tend to work with them for a long time, often for generations.

This is what I've wondered: Is the fact that many families continue to work with the same financial and investing advisors throughout their lifetimes the reason only 3 percent of families lose their family wealth through bad investments and poor legal advice? They don't quit. They don't get one piece of advice and then never talk to the advisor again. They keep on talking, meeting, and working together without interruption. I believe it's because of this constant consultation that these families get the best financial advice available. And it works – at least as far as it can.

But regardless of the competence of their experts, they are unable to overcome the greatest threat to the loss of wealth – the family.

What's the Message?

There's a message here. Let's take a look.

According to study after study, no amount of financial planning will reduce your risk of failure. That's because the root of failure isn't financial. It's usually dysfunctional family dynamics that cause the family to fall apart. Even seemingly minor tensions grow over time into lack of interest, mistrust, and lack of participation so that family ties loosen and good decision-making structures disintegrate. **If families were to put the same kind of relentless effort and commitment into planning for good family relationships as they do into planning for successful financial outcomes, they would beat the odds.** They would have a hugely increased chance of winning.

But families need an overall plan. Not just a financial plan but a strategy for the entire family. They need to get organized. This is the key to success.

When I look at high performance families, it is evident that their success didn't just happen randomly. And it didn't happen because they had a better financial strategy. They've put a lot of effort and time into developing their family relationships and working together to develop policies that would guide them in solving problems, making decisions, and planning for the future. They've been diligently involving all family members so that each one "owns" the plan and commits to upholding the decisions.

They've created a family team that sticks together and values harmony. Together, they look at rising generations as the future hope for the family and accept the challenge of making each individual feel important and valued.

This overall plan is called your *family office strategy.* It's the best way to ensure that your family will succeed long into the future.

Differentiating the Terms

Your family office strategy is your organizational and planning strategy.

Yes, the terminology can get confusing. So let's make it clear. Your overall philosophy and strategy to get organized is your *family office strategy.* It's your umbrella. Within that, you will need to create your *family council* and your *family administrative office.*

You've probably read or heard about a family office before. You may have friends who talk about their family office. This term can be overused and confusing because sometimes the concepts for your overall family office strategy and your family administrative office are not clearly distinguished – even by organizations and institutions that provide family office services.

Family Office Strategy

Family Council

Family Administrative Office

After you commit to developing an overall family office strategy, you should begin to create your family council – because the family council is the control center of your family. Once the family council is in place, you need to decide how to set up your family administrative office as the workforce for your family.

A Paradigm Shift

Historically, high-net-worth families have often set up their family administrative offices first. They realized they needed help managing their investments and all the financial and legal issues that they had to deal with to preserve their wealth. In the past, they didn't understand the connection between family dynamics and loss of wealth. When it looked like they were getting into trouble, they didn't know what else to do, so they doubled down and focused more on their financial capital. It didn't occur to them that human capital – the health and well-being of the individuals in their family – affected their long-term financial success much more than their portfolios.

Only gradually have multigenerational families come to realize the importance of family in maintaining and growing wealth. It's a paradigm shift in our thinking. It requires a cultural change in families to think first of family members and the condition of family dynamics and relationships before contacting a family attorney or wealth advisor.

But the studies make it clear. They corroborate the newspaper headlines you've read and the horror stories you've heard – and conclude that the real key to success is to focus on the family, not on the money.

That's why I recommend creating your family council before you set up your family administrative office. Even though the family administrative office came first in historical development, the family council is first in authority in your family. Decisions about the family and the business of the family emanate from the family council. The family administrative office carries out the directives given to it by the family council.

Starting the Right Way

Larry, a recent client, told me he was aware of other families who had failed and he'd heard lots of stories of family battles that resulted in the family erupting. He vowed he would not let that happen to his family. He was ready to shift his thinking and help get his family organized and ready to prosper. He could already see that, without some good policies and some training in family togetherness, the differences in personalities of his siblings could be a recipe for disaster.

Larry started the right way – with the family council. He recognized it as the foundation of his family. He knew that with the family council in place, he and his family could begin to organize the family administrative office to take care of important financial and legal matters. Together, the family could then decide whether and how they wanted to set up a family bank, a family investment committee, and other entities to meet the family's needs.

The entire family office strategy can seem overwhelming at first. And your family might not need or want every part of the overall strategy. Below is a diagram of how you might eventually organize your family.

Remember, the two main keys to your family's long-term success are the family council and the family administrative office. The rest can be developed over time and as needed.

FAMILY OFFICE STRATEGY

Family Council
(THE ART/THE BRAIN)

A group of family members that make executive decisions for the family as a whole. The Family Council manages all the other qualitative structures.

Family Investment Committee

Headed up by the wealth strategist, the FIC manages and strategizes the family's investments.

Family Administrative Office
(THE SCIENCE/THE BODY)

Handles the day-to-day administration of the trusts, wills, legal documents, day-to-day distributions and loans, family property management.

Family Bank

Administers more significant loans and distributions for the financial stability of family members engaged in productive activities.

Family Constitution

A statement of your family's core beliefs, its values, and more practical considerations, such as how the family aims to manage its wealth and run its business.

Family Mission Statement

Unites the family around a concise description of family values and goals.

Family Education Plan

An organized family program for education and career development of family members.

Family Culture/Brand

A controlled identity that gives your family members a unique advantage and a clearer sense of themselves.

Courtesy of Bonner & Partners Family Office

Separating Two Systems

If you have a family business, of course, it is run by the management and the board of the business, not as an extension of your family. It's important to keep your family system separate from your business system. But at some point, your family members may become involved in the business as the stock of the rising generation converts from non-voting to voting shares, or as business structures shift. At the very least, family members will be interested in your family business. And they *should* be!

But without an organized way to interact with the board or management, family members are likely to cause problems when asking questions or trying to participate. Those in leadership positions in the business are likely to consider family members a nuisance, meddling where they don't belong.

Your family council is the liaison between your family and your business. In teaching family members about the business, how to work together as a team, and how to speak cohesively as one voice, the family council greatly enhances the positive relationships between the family and the business.

Creating the Winning Team

The entire concept of the family office strategy is to make sure your family operates smoothly. But in order to ensure that smooth operation, you need to create a family team – with family members involved and cooperating.

As with any team, you need a coach – a consultant – with a neutral set of eyes to see things family members can't see for themselves. Just as you have experts for your financial and legal lives, you also need an expert for your family life to make sure your family is performing at the optimal level.

Families are the most complex organizations in the world. If they could fix their own problems, they wouldn't just sit by and watch the family crumble. They'd do something about it before it was too late.

So the most successful families keep lifelong family consultants because they know that most families can't recognize and then resolve their own family dynamic issues. If they could, the failure rate wouldn't be so high!

The consultant guides your family, helps to keep it on track, and facilitates the difficult conversations when it gets off track. The consultant acts as a mentor to teach communication and conflict-resolution skills.

Remember, creating a high performance family is like going for the Olympic gold medal. Not many families achieve the goal, but the ones who do have put every effort into achieving success.

One of my clients told me recently, "If I had a medical problem and the doctor told me that I would have a 3 percent chance of survival if I did nothing, but that there is treatment available that almost ensures full recovery for decades to come – with personal effort and the help of a professional – I would definitely choose the latter. So when it comes to getting a coach for my family, I'm totally on board." That's what high performance families do.

It makes sense. A football team doesn't win a few games and then fire the coach, thinking they will get to the Super Bowl on their own. A dance troupe needs the choreographer at every performance to watch for small nuances of misalignment and tiny missteps that take them out of sync. That's how they continue to improve. And a piano player can learn to play the piano from a book, but she'll never get to Carnegie Hall without a coach.

Every winning team needs a coach. And so does a winning family.

The Hesitation

Yet families procrastinate in setting up their family office strategy. Even though you feel the urgency to get your financial and legal issues in order, you may hesitate when it comes to setting up your family council. Here are some of the arguments put forward by some families as to why they hesitated in, or have not yet started, setting up their family office (and some of my counterarguments):

1. **It requires time, effort, and money.** (Yes, it does, because it's a commitment to a *process,* not a one-size-fits-all solution.)

2. **It's a soft structure and there's no immediate bottom line attached to it.** (Correct, you won't see your portfolio jump

immediately to greater heights, but you are protecting both your human and financial capital for the long haul. As studies have shown, families who invest in the family have a much better chance of securing the family wealth.)

3. **We have to get personally involved.** (True, you may have to deal with some emotional issues, but working through these together with your family members will help save your family.)

4. **I think my family can pull off the win without it.** (Maybe that's true, but again, the studies have shown that the odds are definitely against you. It's a big risk to take with your family and your family wealth.)

5. **I'm fighting against a cultural perspective that says seeking help in a psychological realm is a sign of weakness.** (I've heard this many times, but, in fact, it is a sign of strength. Without this help, you're betting on extremely low odds of success, odds you would never agree to in any financial arena of your life.)

In order to ensure your success, you need to employ every advantage you can. By starting with your family council and continuing with your family administrative office, you and your family are training for the Olympics. With continuous commitment to your goals, you'll surely win the gold medal.

Position your family for success by:

1. **Evaluating the benefits of getting organized.**

2. **Making an honest appraisal of your reasons for hesitating.**

3. **Taking a good look at your children and grandchildren.** Your efforts now are a gift to their future prosperity and happiness.

CHAPTER 25

Grow Great Beneficiaries:
Maintaining Excellence in Your Family Trust System

Every year at their annual meeting, the Stanton family sets aside time for each family member to meet privately with their trustees. In between those annual meetings, the trustees invite family members to call them regarding questions about their trusts, concerns for their future, or significant issues that come up in their lives.

This practice has become routine. It's a part of their family culture.

The trustees are responsive and communicative. They're never too busy to connect when a family member reaches out. Sometimes, the trustees initiate contact in order to keep the family members informed of relevant information. They don't always wait for a family meeting, because they want to keep the system open and transparent.

Because of their position in the family office structure, the trustees have intimate information about the family and they understand the needs of each individual family member. But they hold that private information carefully and confidentially. As a result, family members feel comfortable talking with their trustees. They feel heard and respected, and they trust the trustees' advice.

The Stanton family has come to value the strong, positive relationships they have with their trustees. The care and concern their trustees have shown for all members of the family have made an important and positive impact on their personal lives as well as on their financial lives.

It seems ideal. But it wasn't always that way.

The Meteor from Outer Space

The Stanton elders – the trust creators – didn't talk about money. They were tight-lipped and noncommunicative about their estate planning and the trusts for their children and grandchildren. The family members knew they were a part of a very successful family business. Based on how the elder Stantons lived, it was obvious there was a lot of money. But they knew very few details.

What they *did* know was that every December, they received a substantial distribution check from the family company. It wasn't enough for them to live on, but it was big enough to make a difference. The problem was that it arrived like a meteor from outer space, without preparation or explanation, accompanied only by a Merry Christmas note from the family business.[1] The children and grandchildren didn't know whom to thank – or even if they should thank anyone at all.

They weren't sure whether they should feel grateful for the money or guilty for not having earned it. They didn't know the intention of their parents and grandparents in writing the checks, or what they were supposed to do with the money.

Were there strings attached or expectations to be met? Who determined the amount and what metrics were used to determine them? Would they get smaller or larger checks in the future? Could they count on them forever? They were confused and didn't know whom to talk to.

Gifts with No Spirit

Unfortunately, this is not an uncommon scenario. Too often, wealth creators make their estate plans with more concern about solving their tax concerns and protecting their assets than about the impact of the trust distributions on their descendants. Their gifts are

---

1. Meteor metaphor from *The Cycle of the Gift: Family Wealth and Wisdom;* James E . Hughes, Susan E. Massenzio, Keith Whitaker. (Wiley, 2013).

sterile – like payouts from annuities rather than gifts given in the spirit of love and concern for the recipients' well-being. Gifts devoid of feeling and caring are purely quantitative. They undermine the ambitions and passions of the recipients and leave them entitled and dependent. Recipients feel controlled, experiencing the long reach of their parents' power deep within their personal goals and decisions. Rather than enhancing their lives and providing them with opportunities for growth and experience in life, recipients feel pressed down and obligated. Instead of feeling excitement to follow their own dreams, they feel compelled to follow the dreams of their parents.

These are the gifts that backfire because they are given with no conversation about the loving intentions of the giver and no understanding of the needs of the recipients. In their book *Family Trusts: A Guide for Beneficiaries, Trustees, Trust Protectors, and Trust Creators*, authors Hartley Goldstone, James E. Hughes Jr., and Keith Whitaker report that, because of the sterile and controlling context in which many trust distributions are made, 80 percent of beneficiaries consider their trusts to be a burden. Only 10 percent think of them as blessings, and 10 percent are unsure.

As the authors of *Family Trusts* point out,

> "If the fundamental responsibility of each of us, when we touch another, is to do no harm – and it is – then how truly sad it is that 80 percent of trust beneficiaries count their trusts as burdens rather than blessings, especially when 90 percent of a family's financial capital will likely end up in trust. Clearly, the risk of harm is great."

Qualitative Gifts

The Stanton elders loved their offspring, but they didn't know how to set up trusts that considered the effects upon the beneficiaries. Luckily, they *did* know how to select great trustees, professionals who were trained in either finance or law, so they would be sufficiently knowledgeable and experienced to work with the beneficiaries.

After the family elders passed away, the trustees began to develop more personal relationships with the Stanton children and grandchildren. Rather than considering the trusts to be legal structures that happened to involve people, they began to view them as human relationships that happened to take place in a legal environment (*Family Trusts,* Goldstone, Hughes, and Whitaker).

The trustees set about turning the Stanton "meteors" into blessings.

They held group meetings with the family members, during which they explained the structure of the trusts and encouraged questions. Their goal was that each beneficiary would fully understand their trusts. They created charts that showed the percentages of family business shares owned by each family member and explained why there were differences in those percentages. They wanted to prevent confusion, suspicion, and conflict from the get-go.

They had private meetings with each family branch and each individual to get to know them better. They discussed everything including the family members' lifestyles, goals, financial needs, and specific concerns. They emphasized that they were there to help and to responsibly provide the resources needed to enhance the lives of the beneficiaries, whenever possible.

According to the authors of *Family Trusts,* the highest duty of a trustee is to be committed to the question **"If the trust should end and the assets be distributed to the beneficiaries tomorrow, would the beneficiaries have the knowledge, the maturity, and the competency to receive and steward the funds well?"** Because the Stanton family trustees had had long-standing relationships with the trust creators, whom they considered as much friends as clients, they dedicated themselves to doing everything they could to carry out the wishes of these trust creators. Their goal was that the trusts would promote personal growth in the lives of the beneficiaries, not just produce "trust fund babies."

The Forum in Which to Grow

In order for a family to flourish, the entire trust system should fit smoothly and function well together. In the Stanton family, they started with well-written and sound trusts. To that they added great trustees who all clicked and got along well. The third part of the system would be excellent beneficiaries.

In order to accomplish this, the family needed a forum in which to discuss family and personal financial issues. It's difficult to talk about money and trusts in most circumstances, but it's almost impossible to have these discussions with peers or friends who have never experienced inherited wealth. So the Stanton family council became the place where family members could feel safe talking about money, family issues that could affect the trusts, and their feelings regarding their wealth. This was the forum in which they could grow into great beneficiaries.

I met with the family council regularly. It was a vital group. The family council members were enthusiastic and excited to create a larger sense of family identity. They were eager to learn more about their family business, knowing that, one day, they would be its owners. They wanted to know everything they could about their trusts, realizing that, in the future, they would likely become trustees of their own trusts.

Very early on, we outlined and discussed the responsibilities of excellent beneficiaries (*Family Trusts*, Goldstone, Hughes, and Whitaker):

1. **To gain a clear understanding of each trust** in which they have an interest.

2. **To educate themselves** about all trustee responsibilities.

3. **To understand the trustees' responsibility** to balance wise investments with reasonable distributions.

4. **To understand basic portfolio theory** and the process of asset allocation.

5. **To make sure each trustee represents all beneficiaries.**

6. **To meet regularly with trustees** to discuss personal financial circumstances and personal goals, and review the performance of the trustees.

7. **To become knowledgeable about the family's trust governance structure.**

8. **To attend annual family meetings** and accept appropriate, responsible roles within the family governance system.

9. **To develop a general capacity to understand fiduciary accounting.**

10. **To commit to becoming financially literate.**

11. **To understand compensation packages for trustees** and budgets for the trusts.

But it didn't happen overnight. It was a process. Gradually, they began to tackle the tasks required to become more knowledgeable about their trusts. Each one took the items they felt most comfortable with, researched the topics, and shared the information with the others. And they continued to stay in close contact with their trustees and work with them to help educate the other beneficiaries.

An Environment in Which to Flourish

Throughout many months of family council meetings, we also talked about the higher purpose of their family and more philosophical issues that would guide them in the future. We took care of practical family matters and began to learn more about the family business. And we dealt with several family problems that could have caused damage to family harmony. As a result, the beneficiaries learned communication and conflict-resolution skills.

The key was that, over time, they developed an intimate environment in which people really got to know one another. This allowed them to develop respect and genuine fondness for each other as well as a sense of humility for the kinds of things families must deal with in order to flourish. With great thoughtfulness, sensitivity, and earnestness, they considered each issue that came before them. They realized the value of their family team and didn't allow any one person to take over a position of power. As trust grew among them, they were increasingly able to work through differences of opinion in positive ways.

Here's how the Stanton family members were growing into great beneficiaries:

1. **They were interested and enthusiastic.**

2. **They supported one another in their journeys.**

3. **They took advantage of their family governance structure to become educated.**

Lacking any one of these factors, they would most likely have floundered for a long time.

Most importantly, these beneficiaries have learned how to come together and make decisions with consensus. They have learned how to speak with one voice.

Recently, one of the three trustees told me that they hold the beneficiaries in high regard because they have witnessed firsthand the way they have worked together. It is evident in how the beneficiaries interact with them, and it causes the trustees to pay attention. Now, when one of the beneficiaries approaches a trustee, that trustee knows that the group has done their homework and that they are speaking as one. Their group cohesion has gained them the listening ear and the respect of the trustees. This dynamic has had a powerful effect on how the trustees work with the beneficiaries and how they consider their questions and concerns.

Like every family, the Stantons also have problems that need constant attention. But they have laid a strong foundation, and they are committed to a higher state of functioning. They understand the importance of growing into great beneficiaries. And they are becoming increasingly more responsible and mature, and are therefore better able to integrate their trust assets into a flourishing life.

For excellent guidance on how to design a complex family trust system that integrates values, builds on human relationships, and supports a family's flourishing for decades to come, I recommend *Family Trusts: A Guide for Beneficiaries, Trustees, Trust Protectors, and Trust Creators,* Bloomberg Press, 2015, written by my longtime friend Jay Hughes and his colleagues, Hartley Goldstone and Keith Whitaker. It's readily available on Amazon.

Accessing Your Family's Five Capitals for Success

Sixty-five years ago a young man named Sam fell in love with and married Martha, the woman of his dreams. Their entire lives ahead of them, they optimistically began to plan their future.

It didn't cross their minds that there would be family troubles ahead.

With a strong work ethic and the money he had from his family, Sam began a real estate development company. Over the decades he built hotels, shopping malls, and commercial buildings and grew his business into a $200 million enterprise.

Sam chose intelligent and dedicated people to work for him and developed a loyal team of business associates and employees. He was very diligent and devoted to his business, and as the years went on, his wife Martha became active in the business as well.

For different reasons, neither of them had been nurtured while growing up. Their parents hadn't paid much attention to them, so when they had children of their own, they didn't know how to parent. Their four kids grew up with nannies but spent little time with their parents.

Uninvolved Parents

Sam and Martha were good people – honest, down to earth, involved in their community and philanthropically oriented. They just weren't involved in their children's lives. In fact, they seemed to be involved in everything but their kids' lives.

They didn't play with them, help them with their homework, or go to school events. And they didn't just sit and talk with their kids. They didn't seem to understand that it was their job to make their children feel loved, valued, and important. They didn't know that you cannot delegate your responsibility to parent your children to nannies and babysitters.

They focused on their business and neglected their greatest assets – their children.

To their credit, they treated their employees well – respecting them, showing them care and concern, and taking an interest in their personal lives. They treated their employees like family, but, sadly, they didn't treat their family like family.

The result was that their four children suffered greatly. As they grew older, there was nothing to bond them together. They had little sense of belonging to a family. So they went their separate ways, feeling alone, unnurtured and unsupported.

Over time, one sibling created conflict throughout the family and the business, then severed all ties and walked away. Another became an alcoholic and drug addict and, when confronted, also left the family, bitter and resentful. Two of them threatened lawsuits against other family members. And two of them got deeply involved in prostitution and pornography, ruining their relationships and endangering the family business. Among the four of them, there were six divorces.

These adult children didn't understand or trust one another. They were unable to communicate about important family issues. Therefore, they were not equipped to support or work with each other, either personally or when it came to their business.

The root of all these problems was the lack of active parenting when the children were young. The problems stemmed from the parents but came to bear on the children.

The Secret to Success

The company continued to prosper until both Sam and Martha passed away. Then, with no authority at the helm, and siblings who had weak and damaged relationships, the family business and welfare were severely at risk.

Sam and Martha had been committed to growing their business, but they never understood the value of growing their family. They didn't understand that success is more than a big portfolio. It's greater than a booming bottom line.

We already know that seven out of ten families lose their wealth within three generations – no matter how wisely their money is invested and managed. We strive to be one of the three out of ten families that find the secret to maintaining their wealth for many generations.

The good news is that we know a lot about that secret. We know that it has more to do with your family than your business. That secret lies in how well your family functions.

Not that you couldn't lose everything with bad investments, but the statistics show overwhelmingly that you have very competent people managing that part of your life, and it's very unlikely that you will lose your money through poor legal or financial advice.

Balancing Your Family's Capitals

Like Sam and Martha, I'm sure you want to preserve and grow your financial wealth. But family success depends on five different kinds of capital – financial, human, intellectual, social, and spiritual – and the balance among all five.

Families who focus on financial capital and ignore the other four tend to develop problems in family relationships. Tensions and conflicts among siblings arise. Jealousies and feelings of unfairness crop up, especially after the matriarch and patriarch pass away.

Without tight family relationships and a history of confronting problems and settling misunderstandings and disputes among themselves, siblings become suspicious of one another and grow distrustful. The hope of positive resolution fades away.

These are the families who unravel, destroying not only the family harmony and unity but also the family business and wealth.

By examining each of the five capitals* in your family, you have the opportunity to develop the ones that are not as robust as they should be and put your family on a more secure track for success.

1. **Financial capital** – Financial capital has to do with your assets (and your liabilities). It includes your businesses, cash, stocks and investments, real estate, boats, jewelry, art – anything that is to be found on a net worth statement or a balance sheet. It also includes trusts, wills, insurance policies, or any other structures used to secure or transfer this capital.

     Financial capital allows people to provide for their families and employees, invest in companies, and give philanthropically.

     Sam and Martha focused on their financial capital and made sure that their children and grandchildren were well taken care of financially with shares of stock, regular distributions, and opportunities to make future decisions about their business.

     What they didn't understand is that money is not what makes people happy. And a bigger bottom line doesn't ensure overall prosperity. Research shows that, once our basic needs are met, increased financial success does not bring greater joy or contentment in life.

2. **Human capital** – Human capital refers to the individual well-being of family members. It takes into account how well people are flourishing in their personal lives and includes the support and encouragement of passions, skills, talents, interests, and virtues of these individuals. It has to do with recognizing and helping family members develop their specific characteristics, what makes them tick, and how they are "wired."

Sam and Martha didn't pay much individual attention to their children as they were growing up, so they likely didn't know their kids deeply enough to be able to mentor or guide them.

Parents who care about developing a high level of human capital within their family take the time to understand each of their children individually – what they like and don't like, what they feel and what they think. They accept each child's weaknesses as well as strengths. They celebrate each child for who he or she is as a unique person and then do everything they can to help that child meet his needs, become well-rounded and healthy, and reach his potential.

3. **Intellectual capital** – Intellectual capital is about education and training – both formal and informal. It includes experiential knowledge, emotional intelligence, and insights that have been accumulated throughout life. Learning to trust your "gut" is a part of your intellectual capital as well as any reading, research, or intellectual property in which you've gained expertise and that helps you to make wise decisions.

Only one of Sam and Martha's children finished college although funds were available for all of them to do so. Mostly their education and training came from starting their own businesses and learning from their mistakes. We know this can be the most valuable learning we can ever get, and three of the four were quite successful in their careers.

But sadly, these children never benefited from their parents' knowledge or expertise – from their successes and failures – because Sam and Martha didn't spend the time to mentor or coach them. This was a family of secrecy and no communication. So even though the family business created great financial gain, the children never learned about it because no one talked with them about it.

Families who want to give their kids a leg up in the world talk with their kids, not only about the careers they choose but also about the family business, how to invest wisely, and how to read profit-and-loss statements. They help prepare their children for the world they will be living in so they can be responsible heirs and responsible citizens.

4. **Social capital** – Social capital has to do with relationships and connections to other people – and the health of those relationships – both personally and professionally, inside the family and out. It includes networks of professional organizations, committees and boards we serve on, as well as philanthropic work we do. These relationships accumulate throughout our lives and provide us with important resources, access, knowledge, support, and wisdom and give us the opportunity to express our values by giving back and connecting to our higher purpose.

   Sam and Martha were widely connected and had strong relationships with people outside the family. These connections were very important to their lives, both personally and in their business, but they neglected to develop strong, bonded relationships within their family.

   Strong relationships begin at home. Parents who want to give their children the greatest chance for success start by modeling and promoting healthy interactions among family members. In talking with your kids and having family discussions, children learn how to express themselves articulately and appropriately, confront sensitive issues, negotiate and compromise, and solve problems. When children learn to do this at home, they are equipped to do it outside the home – in personal relationships, work situations, and professional organizations.

5. **Spiritual capital** – Spiritual capital refers to one's values, purpose, and faith. It serves as a moral compass to guide you or a navigation tool to direct your behavior and your decisions. It in-

cludes your fundamental beliefs; your good works; your religious and spiritual traditions and practices such as prayer, meditation, moments of flow (when you feel at one with the universe), expressions of love, and other manifestations of a meaningful life. It can be religious or secular, but it comes from the core of your being.

Sam and Martha were moral people, but they didn't spend time talking with their children about what they believed or what drove their decisions. They didn't talk about values, goals, or the meaning of life. Their kids were left to observe and figure it out on their own. Without active parenting to guide and teach them, they made a lot of bad decisions.

Spiritual capital may be the most difficult to measure and the most nebulous to embrace. Yet it may be the most important of all because it lies at the very heart of every family. Spiritual capital drives the soul of your family and sets the tone for your family culture, mission statement, and purpose. Out of your spiritual capital flows your family legacy and what you will pass down to your descendants.

Real Success

Sam and Martha created huge financial capital, but they neglected the other four capitals. And the family endured pain and unhappiness as a result.

In order to avoid the mistake of Sam and Martha, try evaluating your family's capitals by answering each of the questions below. List the specific actions you are already taking and the ones you can implement to make your family stronger in each area.

1. **How much time do you spend with each of your children** getting to know them as individuals and supporting their unique talents and interests? (human capital)

189

2. **What are you doing to prepare your children** to be educated heirs, informed beneficiaries, and responsible citizens in their world? (intellectual capital)

3. **In what ways are you developing and improving the quality of the relationships among your family members** and introducing your children to networking systems outside the family that will be beneficial to them both professionally and personally? (social capital)

4. **How well are you establishing family values and a family culture** that will guide your children's behavior and decisions now and into the future? (spiritual capital)

As parents, you're the ones who have the ability to make the greatest contribution to the success of the people you love most. The health and well-being of your family is a bigger gestalt than just a strong financial situation. It's a more holistic concept. It relies not only on your family's financial wealth but also on its human wealth, intellectual wealth, social wealth, and spiritual wealth. These are the areas that make your family really successful, and these are the areas that bring deep contentment, joy, and happiness.

---

* The work of James E. Hughes Jr. introduced the concept of the four capitals (human, intellectual, social, and financial) in his book *Family Wealth: Keeping It in the Family* (2004). The concept was further expanded to include a fifth capital (spiritual) by Charles Collier, in his book *Wealth in Families* (2006), and by Dennis Jaffe PhD, in various articles. The above descriptions of the five capitals are adapted from Richard Orlando, PhD, of *Legacy Capitals*.

ABOUT THE AUTHOR

Joanne K. Stern, PhD, is a family consultant with an extensive background in psychology. She helps families resolve the complex people problems that often tear families apart and destroy harmony, happiness, and sustained financial success.

A partner at Aspen Consulting Team, Joanne works with entire family systems, couples, and also individuals to settle conflicts in family dynamics, difficulties among siblings, and painful emotional issues. As the family relationships strategic partner for Bonner & Partners, she helps clients around the world resolve their most difficult relationship and communication issues. She writes regularly in the *Bonner & Partners Family Office* monthly newsletter and has conducted workshops at its global investment conferences.

Dr. Stern has had a private psychotherapy practice and has taught college-level parenting courses. She has consulted with businesses and nonprofits both nationally and internationally and has helped career women capitalize on their leadership skills. A frequent speaker, keynote presenter, and workshop leader, she has been a guest expert on more than 200 TV and radio shows and has contributed to various newspapers, magazines, and online media.

She holds a bachelor's and a master's degree from Northwestern University, a double master's in counseling psychology and theology from Fuller Theological Seminary, and a PhD in human and organizational systems from Fielding Graduate University. She has also written *Parenting Is a Contact Sport: 8 Ways to Stay Connected to Your Kids for Life*.

Joanne would love to hear from you at joannestern@gmail.com, or you can contact her through her website at www.aspenconsultingteam.com.

ABOUT BONNER & PARTNERS

Bonner & Partners is an independent research group for individuals and families who want to build wealth and preserve it over the long term.

The group is chaired by Bill Bonner, the founder and president of Agora Inc., the editor of the daily contrarian newsletter *Diary of a Rogue Economist,* and the author of three *New York Times* bestselling books on the financial crisis.

He is joined by his eldest son, Will Bonner, the group's publisher, and a network of dozens of analysts stationed around the world.

To learn more, please visit www.bonnerandpartners.com.

Made in United States
North Haven, CT
23 February 2022

16386001R00115